Edmund S. Morgan, the editor of this volume, is currently Professor of History at Yale University. Dr. Morgan, a recognized expert in his field, is the author of several authoritative books on early American history, among them: *The Birth of the Republic* and *The Stamp Act Crisis.*

THE AMERICAN REVOLUTION:

TWO CENTURIES OF INTERPRETATION

* * * * * *Edited by Edmund S. Morgan*

Prentice-Hall, Inc., *Englewood Cliffs, N.J.*

Current printing (last digit):
11 10 9 8 7 6 5

 Library of Congress Catalog Card Number 65-26857. Printed in the United States of America—C. P 02940, C 02941

CONTENTS

THE AMERICAN REVOLUTION

INTERPRETING THE AMERICAN REVOLUTION

A revolution is a change in human society so large that no one quite understands it, either at the time of its happening or subsequently. Historians seldom agree either about the significance of any particular revolution or about its causes or results. They do not even agree on what the word means or when to employ it. But probably not one would deny that of all the social and political upheavals of the past two centuries, none have affected the western world more profoundly than the American, the French, and the Russian Revolutions. The changes wrought by these three episodes were of such magnitude and complexity that they continue to challenge our understanding not only of the past but of the present: as our understanding of them grows we gain new insights into our own times; and as our own times change we discover new meanings in these revolutions.

Of the three, the American Revolution appears on the surface to have been the simplest, a case merely of the successful resistance by American colonists to the tightening of imperial controls that had previously been loosely and lightly exercised. But if the colonists had done nothing more than defeat a new British colonial policy, their efforts would not be remembered as the American Revolution. Though they did not initially aim at independence, they did achieve it and in doing so became engulfed in other changes that also went beyond their intentions.

Precisely what those changes were is as difficult to determine for the American Revolution as it is for the French and Russian, for a little close inspection reveals such a tangle of forces at work that even the most obvious change cannot be explained by any simple cause. How did the rebellion of thirteen diverse and quarrelsome colonies produce a single nation? How did what looked to many like a crass attempt at tax evasion eventuate in a movement of such high purpose that it could command the devotion of a Washington, a Franklin, a Jefferson, and a John Adams? Even the participants in the Revolution stood in some awe of the forces that swept them. "It seemed," David Ramsay said, "as if the war not only required, but created talents. Men whose minds were warmed with the love of liberty, and whose abilities were improved by daily exercise, and sharpened with a laudable ambition to serve their distressed country, spoke, wrote, and acted, with an energy far surpassing all expectations which could be reasonably founded on their previous acquirements."

In the effort to understand the American Revolution, the earliest historians concentrated on the events leading up to it and showed the unconstitutionality, inequity, and novelty of the series of measures taken by the British toward the colonies from 1763 to 1774. Many later historians have sought to demonstrate the constitutionality, equity, and regularity of those measures and have looked farther back in the colonial past for another explanation of the Revolution. They have discovered motives, trends, and aspirations of which the colonists themselves may not have been fully conscious until they came to the fore after 1776.

In the first selection that follows, David Ramsay, writing in the year when the United States Constitution was adopted, offers a surprisingly objective and penetrating comment on the events through which he had lived during the preceding quarter century. Next, a foreign observer, Friedrich Gentz, summarizes the events leading to the Revolution, in a vein very flattering to the Americans, who proceeded to work the same vein themselves during most of the nineteenth century. That century prided itself on its dedication to liberty, and Americans delighted in tracing their own liberty to the spirit of '76, with Great Britain playing the role of tyrant. This view, frequently designated as the "Whig" interpretation, found its most eloquent spokesman in George Bancroft, a New

Englander who published his great *History of the United States* volume by volume, from 1834 to 1874.

By the end of the century, Anglo-American animosities had cooled, and the golden age of liberty appeared to be veering toward a gilded age of plutocracy and poverty. At this juncture the professional academic historian appeared on the scene and began his minute examination of the American past. Whether he sympathized with Labor or with Capital in the contests of his own day, he was likely to see in the American Revolution something more than a contest between liberty-loving colonists and tyrannizing Englishmen. C. K. Adams in 1898 stressed the internal conflicts among Americans and the corruption and incompetence of the Continental Congress. Subsequent historians, perhaps reflecting on the divisions in their own society, made a good deal more of those conflicts; and J. Franklin Jameson in 1926 found that the Revolution had meant, among other things, a rising of the lower classes to a position of greater economic, social, and political power. Jameson thought that the American and French Revolutions bore a closer resemblance than Americans had previously recognized. His views have been widely influential, but they have not gone unchallenged. Daniel J. Boorstin, writing in 1952, found the significance of the Revolution less in its social changes than in its preservation of institutions inherited from the British.

Meanwhile, the relationship of the Revolution to British institutions had also been studied from other perspectives. British historians, reexamining eighteenth-century politics, discovered that George III was not the would-be tyrant of tradition but an earnest, if not very clever, politician, working hard at the job which the British constitution of the time assigned to him. And American historians began to view the colonial past not simply as a prelude to independence but in the larger context of the British Empire. In doing so, they found much to commend in England's "Old Colonial System" and therefore approached the American Revolution with more sympathy for the problems which the king and his ministers had faced in administering a world-wide empire. The new British point of view is represented here by Eric Robson and that of the American "imperial" historians by Lawrence Henry Gipson.

The old Whig interpretation had actually minimized the significance of the Revolution by maximizing the virtue of those who carried it out and the villainy of those who opposed it. The new interpretations have all expanded our understanding of the Revolution, but they have also presented us with new problems, some of which are suggested in the final selection.

All these essays attempt to get at the essential meaning of the Revolution, but the purpose of the volume is not simply to furnish clues to that meaning or to the changing approaches to it over the past two centuries. The purpose is also to show that the Revolution still offers a challenge to anyone who would understand America either past or present. We come closer to understanding as historians examine the Revolution from new perspectives, gain new insights, and discover forgotten events and trends. But history does not yield all its secrets to anyone, and the Revolution remains at once the most significant and the most elusive episode in our national history. By weighing the arguments offered in the ensuing pages, by measuring them against each other and against the facts, the reader approaching the Revolution for the first time may become aware of its complexity and diversity, and of the challenge it offers to his understanding of his country, his times, and himself.

1.

DAVID RAMSAY

The leaders of the American Revolution, though profoundly impressed with the historical significance of their achievement, had surprisingly little to say about it in writing. When they did, they often spoke enigmatically. Benjamin Rush, a Philadelphia physician who had served in the Continental Congress, declared in 1787: "The American war is over: but this is far from being the case with the American revolution. On the contrary, nothing but the first act of the great drama is closed." But John Adams, a contemporary and friend of Rush, reflecting on the great events of his youth, believed that "The Revolution was effected before the war commenced. The Revolution was in the minds and hearts of the people."

Perhaps the most thoughtful assessment of the Revolution by one of the participants was David Ramsay's History of the American Revolution *(Philadelphia, 1789). Ramsay (1749-1815) was born in Pennsylvania, graduated from Princeton in 1765 and settled in South Carolina. There he practiced both medicine and politics, serving as the state's representative in the Continental Congress 1782-83 and 1785-86. Like other early historians of the Revolution, he relied heavily for factual data on the summaries of events contained in the* Annual Register, *a British periodical that summarized the news year by year. But Ramsay's interpretations were his own, and in the view of one recent scholar they penetrated fur-*

ther into the essential meaning of the Revolution than the more arduous researches of twentieth-century historians have done. The following is one of the most extended passages of interpretation in Ramsay's history. His gloomy view of the moral effects of the Revolution was shared by many—though probably not by most—of the Revolutionary leaders during the 1780s. (Reprinted from David Ramsay, The History of the American Revolution, *Philadelphia, 1789, Volume II, appendix 4, pp. 310-25. In this selection punctuation has been modernized by the elimination of superfluous commas.)*

The state of parties; the advantages and disadvantages of the Revolution; its influence on the minds and morals of the citizens.

Previous to the American revolution, the inhabitants of the British colonies were universally loyal. That three millions of such subjects should break through all former attachments, and unanimously adopt new ones, could not reasonably be expected. The revolution had its enemies, as well as its friends, in every period of the war. Country religion, local policy, as well as private views, operated in disposing the inhabitants to take different sides. The New England provinces being mostly settled by one sort of people, were nearly of one sentiment. The influence of placemen in Boston, together with the connexions which they had formed by marriages, had attached sundry influential characters in that capital to the British interest, but these were but as the dust in the balance, when compared with the numerous independent whig yeomanry of the country. The same and other causes produced a large number in New York, who were attached to royal government. That city had long been head quarters of the British army in America, and many intermarriages, and other connexions, had been made between British officers and some of their first families. The practice of entailing estates had prevailed in New York to a much greater extent than in any of the other provinces. The governors thereof had long been in the habit of indulging their favorites with extravagant grants of land. This had introduced the distinction of landlord and tenant. There was therefore in New York an aristocratic party, respectable for numbers, wealth and influence, which had much to fear from independence. The city was also divided into parties by the influence of two ancient and numerous families, the Livingstones and Delanceys. These having been long accustomed to oppose each other at elections, could rarely be brought to unite in any political measures. In this controversy, one almost universally took part with America, the other with Great Britain.

The Irish in America, with a few exceptions were attached to independence. They had fled from oppression in their native country, and could not brook the idea that it should follow them. Their national prepossessions in favour of liberty were strengthened by their religious opinions. They were Presbyterians, and people of that denomination, for reasons hereafter to be explained, were mostly whigs. The Scotch on the other hand, though they had formerly sacrificed much to liberty in their own country, were generally disposed to support the claims of Great Britain. Their nation for some years past had experienced a large proportion of royal favour. A very absurd association was made by many between the cause of John Wilkes and the cause of America. The former had rendered himself so universally odious to the Scotch, that many of them were prejudiced against a cause which was so ridiculously, but generally associated, with that of a man who had grossly insulted their whole nation. The illiberal reflections cast by some Americans on the whole body of the Scotch, as favourers of arbitrary power, restrained high spirited individuals of that nation from joining a people who suspected their love of liberty. Such of them as adhered to the cause of independence were steady in their attachment. The army and the Congress ranked among their best officers, and most valuable members, some individuals of that nation.

Such of the Germans in America, as possessed the means of information, were generally determined whigs, but many of them were too little informed, to be able to chuse their side on proper ground. They, especially such of them as resided in the interior country, were from their not understanding the English language, far behind most of the other inhabitants, in a knowledge of the merits of the dispute. Their disaffection was rather passive than active: A considerable part of it arose from principles of religion, for some of their sects deny the lawfulness of war. No people have prospered more in America than the Germans. None have surpassed, and but few have equalled them, in industry and other republican virtues.

The great body of tories in the southern states was among the settlers on their western frontier. Many of these were disorderly persons, who had fled from the old settlements to avoid the restraints of civil government. Their numbers were encreased by a set of men called regulators. The expence and difficulty of obtaining the decision of courts, against horse-thieves and other criminals, had induced sundry persons, about the year 1770, to take the execution of the laws into their own hands in some of the remote settlements both of North and South Carolina. In punishing crimes forms as well as substance must be regarded. From not attending to the former some of these regulators, though perhaps aiming at nothing but what they thought right, committed many offences both against law and justice. By their violent proceedings regular government was prostrated. This drew on them the vengeance of royal governors. The regulators having suffered from their hands were slow to oppose an established government whose power to punish they had recently experienced. Apprehending that the measures of Congress were like their own regulating schemes, and fearing that they would terminate in the same disagreeable consequences, they and their adherents were generally opposed to the revolution.

Religion also divided the inhabitants of America. The presbyterians and independents were almost universally attached to the measures of Congress. Their religious societies are governed on the republican plan.

From independence they had much to hope, but from Great Britain if finally successful, they had reason to fear the establishment of a church hierarchy. Most of the episcopal ministers of the northern provinces were pensioners on the bounty of the British government. The greatest part of their clergy, and many of their laity in these provinces, were therefore disposed to support a connexion with Great Britain. The episcopal clergy in these southern provinces being under no such bias, were often among the warmest whigs. Some of them, foreseeing the downfall of religious establishments from the success of the Americans, were less active, but in general where their church was able to support itself, their clergy and laity zealously espoused the cause of independence. Great pains were taken to persuade them that those who had been called dissenters were aiming to abolish the episcopal establishment to make way for their own exaltation, but the good sense of the people restrained them from giving any credit to the unfounded suggestion. Religious controversy was happily kept out of view: The well informed of all denominations were convinced that the contest was for their civil rights, and therefore did not suffer any other considerations to interfere or disturb their union.

The quakers with a few exceptions were averse to independence. In Pennsylvania they were numerous, and had power in their hands. Revolutions in government are rarely patronised by any body of men who foresee that a diminution of their own importance is likely to result from the change. Quakers from religious principles were averse to war, and therefore could not be friendly to a revolution, which could only be effected by the sword. Several individuals separated from them on account of their principles, and following the impulse of their inclinations, joined their countrymen in arms. The services America received from two of their society, generals Greene and Mifflin, made some amends for the embarrassment which the disaffection of the great body of their people occasioned to the exertions of the active friends of independence.

The age and temperament of individuals had often an influence in fixing their political character. Old men were seldom warm whigs. They could not relish the great changes which were daily taking place. Attached to ancient forms and habits, they could not readily accommodate themselves to new systems. Few of the very rich were active in forwarding the revolution. This was remarkably the case in the eastern and middle States; but the reverse took place in the southern extreme of the confederacy. There were in no part of America more determined whigs than the opulent slaveholders in Virginia, the Carolinas and Georgia. The active and spirited part of the community, who felt themselves possessed of talents that would raise them to eminence in a free government, longed for the establishment of independent constitutions: But those who were in possession or expectation of royal favour, or of promotion from Great Britain, wished that the connexion between the Parent State and the colonies might be preserved. The young, the ardent, the ambitious and the enterprising were mostly whigs, but the phlegmatic, the timid, the interested and those who wanted decision were, in general, favourers of Great Britain, or at least only the lukewarm inactive friends of independence. The whigs received a great reinforcement from the operation of continental money. In the year 1775, 1776, and in the first months of 1777, while the bills of Congress were in good credit, the effects of them were the same as if a foreign power had made the United States a present of twenty millions of silver dollars. The circulation of so large a sum of money, and the employment given to great numbers in providing for the American army, increased the numbers and invigorated the zeal of the friends to the revolution: on the same principles the American war was patronised in England by the many contractors and agents for transporting and supplying the British army. In both cases the inconveniences of interrupted commerce were lessened by the employment which war and a domestic circulation of money substituted in its room. The convulsions of war afforded excellent shelter for desperate debtors. The spirit of the times revolted against dragging to jails for debt men who were active and zealous in defending their country, and on the other hand, those who owed more than they were worth, by going within the British lines, and giving themselves the merit of suffering on the score of loyalty, not only put their creditors to defiance, but sometimes obtained promotion or other special marks of royal favour.

The American revolution, on the one hand, brought forth great vices; but on the other hand, it called forth many virtues, and gave occasion for the display of abilities which, but for that event, would have been lost to the world. When the war began, the Americans were a mass of husbandmen, merchants, mechanics and fishermen; but the necessities of the country gave a spring to the active powers of the inhabitants, and set them on thinking, speaking and acting, in a line far beyond that to which they had been accustomed. The difference between nations is not so much owing to nature as to education and circumstances. While the Americans were guided by the leading strings of the mother country, they had no scope nor encouragement for exertion. All the departments of government were established and executed for them, but not by them. In the years 1775 and 1776, the country, being suddenly thrown into a situation that needed the abilities of all its sons, these generally took their places, each according to the bent of his inclination. As they severally pursued their objects with ardor, a vast expansion of the human mind speedily followed. This displayed itself in a variety of ways. It was found that the talents for great stations did not differ in kind, but only in degree, from those which were necessary for the proper discharge of the ordinary business of civil society. In the bustle that was occasioned by the war, few instances could be produced of any persons who made a figure, or who rendered essential services, but from among those who had given specimens of similar talents in their respective professions. Those who from indolence or dissipation had been of little service to the community in time of peace were found equally unserviceable in war. A few young men were exceptions to this general rule. Some of these, who had indulgd in youthful follies, broke off from their vicious courses, and on the pressing call of their country became useful servants of the public: but the great bulk of those who were the active instruments of carrying on the revolution, were self-made, industrious men. These, who by their own exertions had established or laid a foundation for establishing personal independence, were most generally trusted, and most successfully employed in establishing that of their country. In these times of action, classical education was found of less service than good natural parts, guided by common sense and sound judgement.

Several names could be mentioned of individuals who, without the knowledge of any other language than their mother tongue, wrote not only accurately, but elegantly, on public business. It seemed as if the war not only required, but created talents. Men whose minds were warmed with the love of liberty, and whose abilities were improved by daily exercise, and sharpened with a laudable ambition to serve their distressed country, spoke, wrote, and acted, with an energy far surpassing all expectations which could be reasonably founded on their previous acquirements.

The Americans knew but little of one another previous to the revolution. Trade and business had brought the inhabitants of their seaports acquainted with each other, but the bulk of the people in the interior country were unacquainted with their fellow citizens. A continental army and Congress composed of men from all the States, by freely mixing together, were assimilated into one mass.

Individuals of both, mingling with the citizens, disseminated principles of union among them. Local prejudices abated. By frequent collision asperities were worn off, and a foundation was laid for the establishment of a nation out of discordant materials. Intermarriages between men and women of different States were much more common than before the war, and became an additional cement to the union. Unreasonable jealousies had existed between the inhabitants of the eastern and of the southern States; but on becoming better acquainted with each other, these in a great measure subsided. A wiser policy prevailed. Men of liberal minds led the way in discouraging local distinctions, and the great body of the people, as soon as reason got the better of prejudice, found that their best interests would be most effectually promoted by such practices and sentiments as were favourable to union. Religious bigotry had broken in upon the peace of various sects before the American war. This was kept up by partial establishments, and by a dread that the church of England through the power of the mother country would be made to triumph over all other denominations. These apprehensions were done away by the revolution. The different sects, having nothing to fear from each other, dismissed all religious controversy. A proposal for introducing bishops into America before the war had kindled a flame among the dissenters; but the revolution was no sooner accomplished, than a scheme for that purpose was perfected with the consent and approbation of all those sects who had previously opposed it. Pulpits which had formerly been shut to worthy men because their heads had not been consecrated by the imposition of the hands of a Bishop, or of a Presbytery, have since the establishment of independence been reciprocally opened to each other whensoever the public convenience required it. The world will soon see the result of an experiment in politics, and be able to determine whether the happiness of society is increased by religious establishments, or diminished by the want of them.

Though schools and colleges were generally shut up during the war, yet many of the arts and sciences were promoted by it. The Geography of the United States before the revolution was but little known; but the marches of armies and the operations of war gave birth to many geographical enquiries and discoveries, which otherwise would not have been made. A passionate fondness for studies of this kind, and the growing importance of the country, excited one of its sons, the Rev. Mr. Morse, to travel through every State of the Union, and amass a fund of topographical knowledge far exceeding any thing heretofore communicated to the public. The necessities of the States led to the study of Tactics, Fortification, Gunnery, and a variety of other arts connected with war, and diffused a knowledge of them among a peaceable people who would otherwise have had no inducement to study them.

The abilities of ingenious men were directed to make farther improvements in the art of destroying an enemy. Among these, David Bushnell of Connecticut invented a machine for submarine navigation which was found to answer the purpose of rowing horizontally at any given depth under water, and of rising or sinking at pleasure. To this was attached a magazine of powder, and the whole was contrived in such a manner as to make it practicable to blow up vessels by machinery under them. Mr. Bushnell also contrived sundry other curious machines for the annoyance of British shipping; but from accident they only succeeded in part. He destroyed one vessel in charge of commodore Symonds, and a second one near the shore of Long Island.

Surgery was one of the arts which was promoted by the war. From the want of hospitals and other aids, the medical men of America had few opportunities of perfecting themselves in this art, the thorough knowledge of which can only be acquired by practice and observation. The melancholy events of battles gave the American students an opportunity of seeing and learning more in one day than they could have acquired in years of peace. It was in the hospitals of the United States that Dr. Rush first discovered the method of curing the lockjaw by bark and wine, added to other invigorating remedies, which has since been adopted with success in Europe as well as in the United States.

The science of government has been more generally diffused among the Americans by means of the revolution. The policy of Great Britain in throwing them out of her protection induced a necessity of establishing independent constitutions. This led to reading and reasoning on the subject. The many errors that were at first committed by unexperienced statesmen have been a practical comment on the folly of unbalanced constitutions and injudicious laws. The discussions concerning the new constitution gave birth to much reasoning on the subject of government, and particularly to a series of letters signed "Publius," but really the work of Alexander Hamilton, in which much political knowledge and wisdom were displayed, and which will long remain a monument of the strength and acuteness of the human understanding in investigating truth.

When Great Britain first began her encroachments on the colonies, there were few natives of America who had distinguished themselves as speakers or writers, but the controversy between the two countries multiplied their number.

The stamp act, which was to have taken place in 1765, employed the pens and tongues of many of the colonists, and by repeated exercise improved their ability to serve their country. The duties imposed in 1767 called forth the pen of John Dickinson, who in a series of letters signed "a Pennsylvania Farmer," may be said to have sown the seeds of the revolution. For being universally read by the colonists, they universally enlightened them on the dangerous consequences likely to result from their being taxed by the parliament of Great Britain.

In establishing American independence, the pen and the press had merit equal to that of the sword. As the war was the people's war and was carried on without funds, the exertions of the army would have been insufficient to effect the revolution, unless the great body of the people had been prepared for it and also kept in a constant disposition to oppose Great Britain. To rouse and unite the inhabitants and to persuade them to patience for several years, under present sufferings, with the hope of obtaining remote advantages for their posterity, was a work of difficulty: This was effected in a great measure by the tongues and pens of the well informed citizens, and on it depended the success of military operations.

To enumerate the names of all those who were successful labourers in this arduous business, is impossible. The following list contains, in nearly alphabetical order, the names of the most distingushed writers in favour of the rights of America.

John Adams, and Samuel Adams, of Boston; Bland, of Virginia; John Dickinson, of Pennsylvania; Daniel Dulany, of Annapolis; William Henry Drayton, of South Carolina; Dr. Franklin, of Philadelphia; John Jay, and Alexander Hamilton, of New York; Thomas

Jefferson, and Arthur Lee of Virginia; Jonathan Hyman, of Connecticut; Governor Livingston, of New Jersey; Dr. Mayhew, and James Otis, of Boston; Thomas Paine, Dr. Rush, Charles Thompson, and James Wilson, of Philadelphia; William Tennant, of South Carolina; Josiah Quincy, and Dr. Warren, of Boston. These and many others laboured in enlightening their countrymen on the subject of their political interests, and in animating them to a proper line of conduct in defence of their liberties. To these individuals may be added the great body of the clergy, especially in New England. The printers of news papers had also much merit in the same way. Particularly Eedes and Gill, of Boston; Holt, of New York; Bradford, of Philadelphia; and Timothy, of South Carolina.

The early attention which had been paid to literature in New England was also eminently conducive to the success of the Americans in resisting Great Britain. The university of Cambridge was founded as early as 1636, and Yale college in 1700. It has been computed that in the year the Boston port act was passed, there were in the four eastern colonies upwards of two thousand graduates of their colleges dispersed through their several towns, who by their knowledge and abilities were able to influence and direct the great body of the people to a proper line of conduct for opposing the encroachments of Great Britain on their liberties. The colleges to the southward of New England, except that of William and Mary in Virginia, were but of modern date; but they had been of a standing sufficiently long to have trained for public service a considerable number of the youth of the country. The college of New Jersey, which was incorporated about 28 years before the revolution, had in that time educated upwards of 300 persons, who, with a few exceptions, were active and useful friends of independence. From the influence which knowledge had in securing and preserving the liberties of America, the present generation may trace the wise policy of their fathers in erecting schools and colleges. They may also learn that it is their duty to found more, and support all such institutions. Without the advantages derived from these lights of this new world, the United States would probably have fallen in their unequal contest with Great Britain. Union, which was essential to the success of their resistance, could scarcely have taken place in the measures adopted by an ignorant multitude. Much less could wisdom in council, unity in system, or perseverance in the prosecution of a long and self denying war be expected from an uninformed people. It is a well known fact that persons unfriendly to the revolution were always most numerous in those parts of the United States which had either never been illuminated, or but faintly warmed by the rays of science. The uninformed and the misinformed constituted a great proportion of those Americans who preferred the leading strings of the Parent State, though encroaching on their liberties, to a government of their own countrymen and fellow citizens.

As literature had in the first instance favoured the revolution, so in its turn, the revolution promoted literature. The study of eloquence and of the Belles Lettres was more successfully prosecuted in America, after the disputes between Great Britain and her colonies began to be serious, than it ever had been before. The various orations, addresses, letters, dissertations and other literary performances which the war made necessary called forth abilities where they were, and excited the rising generation to study arts, which brought with them their own reward. Many incidents afforded materials for the favourites of the muses to display their talents. Even burlesquing royal proclamations, by parodies and doggerel poetry, had great effects on the minds of the people. A celebrated historian has remarked that the song of Lillibullero forwarded the revolution of 1688 in England. It may be truly affirmed that similar productions produced similar effects in America. Francis Hopkinson rendered essential service to his country by turning the artillery of wit and ridicule on the enemy. Philip Freneau laboured successfully in the same way. Royal proclamations and other productions which issued from royal printing presses were, by the help of a warm imagination, arrayed in such dresses as rendered them truly ridiculous. Trumbull, with a vein of original Hudibrastic humour, diverted his countrymen so much with the follies of their enemies that for a time they forgot the calamities of war. Humphries twined the literary with the military laurel by superadding the fame of an elegant poet to that of an accomplished officer. Barlow increased the fame of his country and of the distinguished actors in the revolution by the bold design of an epic poem ably executed on the idea that Columbus foresaw in vision the great scenes that were to be transacted on the theatre of that new world which he had discovered. Dwight struck out in the same line, and at an early period of life finished an elegant work entitled "the Conquest of Canaan," on a plan which has rarely been attempted. The principles of their mother tongue were first unfolded to the Americans since the revolution by their countryman Webster. Pursuing an unbeaten track, he has made discoveries in the genius and construction of the English language which had escaped the researches of preceding philologists. These and a group of other literary characters have been brought into view by the revolution. It is remarkable that of these, Connecticut has produced an unusual proportion. In that truly republican state every thing conspires to adorn human nature with its highest honours.

From the later periods of the revolution till the present time, schools, colleges, societies, and institutions for promoting literature, arts, manufactures, agriculture, and for extending human happiness, have been increased far beyond any thing that ever took place before the declaration of independence. Every state in the union has done more or less in this way, but Pennsylvania has done the most. The following institutions have been very lately founded in that state, and most of them in the time of the war or since the peace. An university in the city of Philadelphia; a college of physicians in the same place; Dickinson college at Carlisle; Franklin college at Lancaster; the Protestant Episcopal academy in Philadelphia; academies at Yorktown, at Germantown, at Pittsburgh and Washington; and an academy in Philadelphia for young ladies; societies for promoting political enquiries; for the medical relief of the poor under the title of the Philadelphia dispensary; for promoting the abolition of slavery and the relief of free negroes unlawfully held in bondage; for propagating the gospel among the Indians, under the direction of the United Brethren; for the encouragement of manufactures and the useful arts; for alleviating the miseries of prisons. Such have been some of the beneficial effects which have resulted from that expansion of the human mind which has been produced by the revolution, but these have not been without alloy.

To overset an established government unhinges many of those principles which bind individuals to each other. A long time and much prudence will be necessary to reproduce a spirit of union and that reverence for government without which society is a rope of sand. The right of the people to resist their rulers when invading their liberties forms the cornerstone of the American republics. This principle, though just in itself, is not favourable to the tranquillity of present establishments. The maxims and measures, which in the years 1774 and 1775 were successfully inculcated and adopted by American patriots for oversetting the established government, will answer a similar purpose when recurrence is had to them by factious demagogues for disturbing the freest governments that were ever devised.

War never fails to injure the morals of the people engaged in it. The American war, in particular, had an unhappy influence of this kind. Being begun without funds or regular establishments, it could not be carried on without violating private rights; and in its progress it involved a necessity for breaking solemn promises and plighted public faith. The failure of national justice, which was in some degree unavoidable, increased the difficulties of performing private engagements, and weakened that sensibility to the obligations of public and private honor which is a security for the punctual performance of contracts.

In consequence of the war, the institutions of religion have been deranged, the public worship of the Deity suspended, and a great number of the inhabitants deprived of the ordinary means of obtaining that religious knowledge which tames the fierceness and softens the rudeness of human passions and manners. Many of the temples dedicated to the service of the most High, were destroyed, and these, from a deficiency of ability and inclination, are not yet rebuilt. The clergy were left to suffer, without proper support. The depreciation of the paper currency was particularly injurious to them. It reduced their salaries to a pittance, so insufficient for their maintenance that several of them were obliged to lay down their profession and engage in other pursuits. Public preaching, of which many of the inhabitants were thus deprived, seldom fails of rendering essential service to society by civilizing the multitude and forming them to union. No class of citizens have contributed more to the revolution than the clergy, and none have hitherto suffered more in consequence of it. From the diminution of their number, and the penury to which they have been subjected, civil government has lost many of the advantages it formerly derived from the public instructions of that useful order of men.

On the whole, the literary, political, and military talents of the citizens of the United States have been improved by the revolution, but their moral character is inferior to what it formerly was. So great is the change for the worse, that the friends of public order are loudly called upon to exert their utmost abilities in extirpating the vicious principles and habits which have taken deep root during the late convulsions.

2.

FRIEDRICH GENTZ

Nearly every assessment of the American Revolution since 1789 has implicitly or explicitly taken the French Revolution as a point of reference. An attempt to understand one revolution gains from a consideration of the other. One of the earliest extended comparisons was written in 1800 by Friedrich Gentz (1764-1832), a Prussian statesman who later became adviser to Metternich.

Although Gentz extolled the American Revolution in order to castigate the French, he was well informed about the historical developments leading to American independence. In his pages may be found many of the interpretations of events developed at greater length in the earlier works of David Ramsay and the later ones of George Bancroft and George Otto Trevelyan. Gentz was wrong about the details of the Tea Act of 1773, and he exaggerated the terms of the Massachusetts Government Act of 1774, which revised but did not destroy the charter of the colony. He also erred in thinking that the trade regulations of 1764 were concerned only with maintaining the British monopoly of American commerce. The Act of 1764 was cast as a revenue act and resented as such. Moreover, Gentz struck a note not sounded by American writers in his dismissal of the "rights of man." But in other respects his account may stand as an extraordinarily succinct statement of what is commonly called the "Whig" interpretation of the American Revolution.

John Quincy Adams, who knew something of the American Revolution at first hand, was serving as American minister to Prussia when Gentz's account appeared. Adams was so impressed that he translated it and published it in Philadelphia. The selection that follows, in Adams's translation and with his foreword, constitutes more than half of this seventy-three-page book. (Reprinted from Friedrich Gentz, The Origin and Principles of the American Revolution, Compared with the Origin and Principles of the French Revolution, *translated "by an American Gentleman" [i.e., John Quincy Adams], Philadelphia, 1800, pp. 3-41. In this selection, as in the preceding one, punctuation has been modernized by the elimination of superfluous commas.)*

The Origin and Principles of the American Revolution, Compared with the Origin and Principles of the French Revolution

Preface

The essay of which a translation is here given was published in the *Historic Journal,* a monthly print which appears at Berlin; and was written by Mr. GENTZ, one of the most distinguished political writers in Germany. It is for two reasons highly interesting to Americans: First, because it contains the clearest account of the rise and progress of the revolution which established their independence, that has ever appeared within so small a compass; and secondly, because it rescues that revolution from the disgraceful imputation of having proceeded from the same principles as that of France. This error has nowhere been more frequently repeated, nowhere of more pernicious tendency than in America itself. It has been here not simply a commonplace argument, as Mr. Gentz represents it to have been in Europe, but has been sanctioned by the authority of men, revered for their talents, and who at least ought to have known better.

The essential difference between these two great events, in their *rise,* their *progress,* and their *termination,* is here shewn in various lights, one of which alone is sufficient for an honest man. A modern philosopher may contend that the sheriff who executes a criminal, and the highwayman who murders a traveller act upon the same principles; the plain sense of mankind will still see the same difference between them that is here proved between the American and French Revolutions—The difference between *right* and *wrong*.

We presume it will afford a pure and honest gratification to the mind of every truly patriotic American reader, to see the honourable testimony borne by an ingenious, well-informed, and impartial foreigner to the principles and conduct of our country's revolution. The judgment of a native American will naturally be biassed by those partialities in favour of his country, from which it is so difficult for the citizen to divest himself as an historian. The causes of hatred and affection must be more remote from the mind of a foreigner, and his decisions must therefore have a greater intrinsic value. The historian of his own country must always in some sort be considered as its advocate; but an impartial foreigner is its judge.

The approbation of such a writer as Mr. Gentz is the more precious too, for not being unqualified. The mild censure, which he passes upon certain parts of our proceedings is the strongest proof of his real impartiality; and though our sentiments as Americans may differ from his, upon various points of political speculation, we shall find very few, if any instances, that have incurred his censure, which our own candour will not equally disapprove.

Origin and Principles, &c.

The Revolution of North America had, in the course of events, been the nearest neighbour to that of France. A very considerable part of those who were cotemporaries and witnesses of the latter had likewise survived the former. Some of the most important personages who made a figure in the French revolution scarce ten years before had been active on the theatre of that in America. The example of this undertaking, crowned with the most complete success, must have had a more immediate and powerful influence upon those who destroyed the old government of France than the example of any earlier European revolution: the circumstances in which France was, at the breaking out of her revolution, had been, if not wholly, yet for the greatest part brought on by the part she had taken in that of America. In the conduct and language of most of the founders of the French revolution, it was impossible not to perceive an endeavour to imitate the course, the plans, the measures, the forms, and, in part, the language of those who had conducted that of America; and to consider this, upon all occasions, as at once the model and the justification of their own.

From all these causes, but especially because the recollection of the American revolution was yet fresh in every mind; because the principles to which it had given currency still sounded in every ear; because the preparatory temper of mind, which it had everywhere in Europe excited and left behind, favoured every similar or only seemingly similar undertaking, it became so easy for those who felt an evident interest in seeing the French revolution superficially compared, and thereby placed on the same ground and confounded with that of America, to draw the great majority of the public into this fundamentally false point of view. At the period of great commotions and of animated, vehement, widely grasping discussions, a very small number of men are able and, perhaps, a still smaller number willing, with vigorous native energy, to penetrate into the essence of events, and take upon themselves the painful task of forming a judgment founded upon long meditation and persevering study. The similarity of the two revolutions was taken upon trust, and as many persons of respectable understanding and discernment had loudly and decisively declared themselves in favour of the American, it became a sort of accredited common-place, "that what had been just in America, could not be unjust in Europe." As, further, the last result of the American revolution had been in the highest degree splendid and glorious; as its issue had been undoubtedly advantageous for America, undoubtedly advantageous for most other states, was undoubtedly advantageous for England herself; as this most important circumstance and the greater moderation and impartiality which time and tranquillity always bring to the judgments of men had at last reconciled with this revolution its most violent opponents; an irresistable analogy seemed to justify a similar expectation in respect to that of France; and a second common-place, far more dangerous than the first, because it seized its materials in the empty space of distant futurity, gathered a great portion of the human race under the spell of the delusive hope that "what in America had conduced to the public benefit will, and must, sooner or later, in France and throughout Europe conduce in like manner to the public benefit."

The melancholy experience of ten disastrous years has indeed considerably cooled down this belief; but it is not yet altogether extinguished; and even those who have begun to totter in the faith without, however, renouncing the principles by which they justify the French revolution, extricate themselves from their perplexity by recurring to external and accidental circumstances, which have hindered all the good that might have ensued, to the pretence that the revolution is not yet wholly completed, and to other equally nugatory subterfuges. The justice of the origin of both revolutions they suppose to be taken for granted; and if one of them has produced more salutary consequences than the other, they impute this to Fortune, which here favours and there abandons the undertakings of men. An equality of wisdom in the founders of the two revolutions, upon the whole, is as much taken for granted as an equality of integrity.

Hence, it will certainly be no ungrateful task to compare the two revolutions in their essential features, in their originating causes, and in their first principles with each other. But in order to prepare the way for such a comparison, it will not be superfluous to exhibit in a small compass the principal features of the origin of the American revolution. It may justly be taken for granted that since the last ten years have almost exhausted all the powers of attention and of memory, the characteristic features of the origin and first progress of that revolution are no longer distinctly present in the minds even of many of its cotemporaries: there are, besides, some points in the picture of this great event, which, at the time when it happened, escaped almost every observer; and which, not until a later period, discovered themselves in all their vivid colours to the piercing eyes of meditation and experience.[1]

The English colonies in North America, far from being a designed regular institution of European wisdom calculated for futurity, had

[1] Thus, for example, among all the statesmen and literati who spoke or wrote, either for or against the American revolution, there were only two who even then foresaw that the loss of the colonies would be no misfortune to England: The one, Adam Smith, was at that time little read and, perhaps, little understood: The other, Dean Tucker, was held an eccentric visionary.

been much more the pure production of European short-sightedness and injustice. Political and religious intolerance, political and religious convulsions, had driven the first settlers from their country: the single favour indulged them was to leave them to themselves. That their establishments were, in less than two hundred years, to form a great nation, and to give the world a new form, was concealed no less to their own eyes than to the eyes of those who had ejected them from their bosom.

In the apparent insignificance of those settlements, and in the false measure by which the profound ignorance of the Europeans estimated the value of such distant possessions, lay the first ground of the extraordinary progress which the North American colonies had already made under the second and third generations of their new inhabitants. Gold and silver alone could then attract the attention of European governments. A distant land where neither of these was to be found was, without hesitation, abandoned to its fortunes. From such a country was expected no *revenue;* and what increases not immediately the revenues of the state, could make no pretensions to its support, or to its particular care.

Nevertheless, by the peculiar, creative energy of a rapidly growing mass of enterprising and indefatigably active men, favoured by an extensive, fruitful, and happily situated territory; by simple forms of government well adapted to their ends, and by profound peace, these colonies, thus neglected and well nigh forgotten by the mother country sprang up, after a short infancy, with giant strides, to the fulness and consistency of a brilliant youth. The phenomenon of their unexpected greatness roused the Europeans with sudden violence from the slumber of a thoughtless indifference and, at length, displayed to them a real new world, fully prepared to rivalize with the old; for which, however, at the same time, it was an inexhaustible source of wealth and enjoyment. Even before the middle of this century, every maritime power of Europe, but England more than all the rest, because the foundation of her colonies had accidentally departed the least from good principles, had discovered that the peculiar and only worth of all external European possessions consisted in the extended market they opened to the industry of the mother country; that it was not the empty sovereignty over enormous territories; not the barren right of property to gold and silver mines; but solely the encreased facility of sale for European productions, and an advantageous exchange of them for the productions of the most distant regions, which gave to the discovery of America the first rank among all the events beneficial to the world.

No sooner had this great truth begun to be so much as obscurely perceived, than necessarily all the exertions of the mother country concentrated themselves in giving to their trade with the colonies the greatest extent and the most advantageous direction; and for this end, even in times so little remote from the present as those of which I speak, no other means were devised than a *Monopoly.* In compelling the inhabitants of the colonies to receive exclusively from the mother country all the necessary European articles they required, and to sell exclusively to her all the productions by the circulation of which the merchants of the mother country might hope a certain profit, it was supposed [that] that vast market, whose importance became more evident from year to year, would be improved in its whole extent, and under the most profitable conditions.

The error which lay at the bottom of this system was pardonable. The genuine principles of the nature and sources of wealth, and of the true interests of commercial nations had scarcely yet germed in a few distinguished heads, and were not even developed, much less acknowledged. Nay, if at that early period a single state could have soared to the elevation of these principles; on one side, had renounced all prejudices, on the other, every paltry jealousy, and felt a lively conviction that liberty and general competition must be the basis of all true commercial policy, and the wisest principle of trade with the colonies, yet could she not, without sacrificing herself, have listened to this principle. For in leaving her colonies free she would have run the risque of seeing them fall into the hands of another, who would exclude her from their market. She was not privileged to be wise alone, and to have expected a general concert among the commercial powers would have been folly. As therefore a colonial trade grounded upon monopoly was yet better than none, there remained for a state in the situation of England, even had she most fortunately anticipated the result of a long experience and of profound meditation, no other system than that of *monopoly.*

To secure to herself the exclusive trade of the colonies was under these circumstances necessarily the highest aim of England's policy.

The establishment of this exclusive trade, which naturally arose from the original relations between the colonies and the mother country, had not been difficult to the state; for the emigrants had never received the smallest support. By so much the more expensive had it been to keep them. The possession of the colonies was the occasion of wars. The war of eight years between France and England, which concluded in the year 1763 by the peace of Fontainebleau, and which encreased the English national debt nearly an hundred millions sterling, had the colonial interest for its sole object. The conquest of Canada would not in itself have been worth a tenth part of the sums which that war cost; the firm establishment of the commercial monopoly was properly the final purpose for which they were expended.

It is a great question whether even independent of the unhappy differences which broke out immediately after the close of that war, its consequences would not have been rather pernicious than salutary to England. The annihilation of the French power in North America completed the political existence of the English colonies, and supported by the still accelerating progress of their wealth and of their vigor, gave them a consciousness of security and of stability which must have become sooner or later dangerous to their connection with the mother country. It is more than improbable that this connection would have been perpetual. It is difficult to believe that under the most favourable circumstances it would have lasted another century. No nation governed its colonies upon more liberal and equitable principles than England; but the unnatural system which chained the growth of a great people to the exclusive commercial interest of a country distant from them a thousand leagues, even with the most liberal organization of which it was capable, could not have lasted forever.[2] Yet it would certainly have maintained itself for the next fifty years, and might perhaps have been dissolved in a milder and happier way than has now happened, had not England, under the most wretched of fascinations, fallen upon the idea of procuring in addition to the benefit of an exclusive trade, another immediate benefit by an American public revenue.

[2] So long as the colonists had found a paramount advantage in the *culture of the land,* they would probably have borne their dependence. But when the critical period had arrived, when in the natural progress of society a considerable part of the capitals would have been employed in *manufactures,* the English monopoly would have become insupportable.

It is hard to decide which of the secret motives which on either side were imputed to the ministry of that time first gave existence to this pernicious project. The most pardonable of all, the wish of alleviating the burthen of taxes upon the people of Great Britain, and especially upon the land-holders, a burthen which the war had so much aggravated, is unluckily at the same time the most improbable. Specie [coin] was exactly that in which North America least abounded; to have levied in that country a tax of any real importance could scarcely have occurred to any Englishman with the least smattering of information; and that, amidst the thousand obstacles which must necessarily have opposed the collection of such a tax, its net produce for the treasury would always have melted to nothing, could scarcely escape the sagacity of any person versed in the subject. If we consider it attentively on all sides; if we carefully remark certain expressions of the ministers of that day, and what were afterwards known to be their favourite ideas, as well as the whole course of transactions upon American affairs, we can hardly avoid the belief that what is generally considered as the *consequence* of the first treasury plan, the jealousy of the parliament's unlimited supremacy was rather the proper motive for this plan; and the secret apprehension that America might grow weary of her fetters misled them to the dangerous experiment of fastening still narrower chains upon her.

The first step in this untrodden career was taken immediately after the peace of 1763, and under the most unfavourable auspices. The minister of finance, George Grenville, else in every respect an estimable and excellent statesman, but whose mind was either not great or not flexible enough to consider the new system in all its points of view, thought he could force down its execution just at the period when, by various severe acts of parliament, he had brought back the commercial relations between England and the colonies as close as possible to the principles of monopoly; had pursued the American contraband trade, with the most oppressive regulations, and thereby had excited a great discontent in all minds. The tax with which he proposed to make his first essay was a stamp-tax upon judicial records, newspapers, &c. to which the parliament, at the commencement of the year 1765, gave its assent.

The colonies had hitherto paid no other taxes than those which were necessary for the internal administration; and these proportionably insignificant charges had been prescribed and assessed by the several representative assemblies of each colony. In cases of urgency, for instance, in the course of the late war, these assemblies had raised and presented to the government extraordinary and voluntary contributions; but of a public tax, raised by act of parliament, there had been in North America no example. If the parliament in the laws regulating trade had sometimes introduced a trifling entrance, or clearance duty, the most distant trace had never appeared in any public transaction of a design to make America contribute immediately to the general exigencies of the British empire.

A long and venerable *observance* had sanctioned this colonial immunity; a thousand equitable considerations, and this above all, that the British commercial monopoly was of itself equivalent to a heavy and invaluable tax, justified this observance; and what was most important of all, even the authority of the parliament to violate this immunity was controvertible with weapons furnished by the spirit of the English constitution itself. It had always been a favourite maxim of this constitution that no Briton could be compelled to pay taxes not imposed by his own representatives, and upon this maxim rested the whole constitutional power of the lower house in parliament. That the inhabitants of the colonies, in every sense of the word, were Britons, no man questioned; and the parliament, which thought itself authorised to tax them, even in that, recognized them as fellow citizens. Yet had they no representatives in parliament and, owing to their distance, could properly make no pretensions to it. If, therefore, in respect to them, the constitutional principle retained its force, their contributions could only be prescribed by their colonial assemblies, and the British parliament was no more entitled to exercise the right of taxation over them than over the people of Ireland.

But had this right been only questionable, it was at all events a false and hazardous step to bring it into discussion. To raise a controversy concerning the bounds of the supreme power in the state, without the most urgent necessity, is in every case contrary to the simplest rules of state policy. Doubly dangerous must such a controversy here be, where it concerned a constitution whose nature and boundaries had never yet been defined and were, perhaps, not susceptible of definition. The relation between a colony and the mother country is one of those which will not bear a strong elucidation; rights of sovereignty of so peculiar and extraordinary a nature often vanish under the hands of those who would dissect them. Now, when the mother country has a constitution like that of Britain, it becomes infinitely difficult to introduce into that relation a harmony which satisfies the understanding, and at the same time the idea of right. It had never been examined how far the legislative authority of parliament in respect to the colonies extended; thus much, however, the colonies admitted, and would have continued long to admit, that the parliament was fully authorised to direct and to restrain their trade in the widest extent of the word. This alone was clear; but this alone was essential to England. An attempt to go further was manifestly to set all at stake.

The appearance of the stamp-act in America was the signal for an universal commotion. The new laws against contraband trade had already irritated the minds of the people, because they plainly manifested the purpose of maintaining the British commercial monopoly in its greatest vigour; but these laws were received in silence, because there was no pretention to the right of complaining against them. Now, a new and hitherto unexampled system, that of raising in North America a tax for the treasury of England, was to be introduced, and in a form necessarily odious to the colonies; for a stamp-tax, from various local causes, had always been in North America an oppressive tax. The opposition spread in a few days among all classes of people; in the lower, it burst forth in excesses of every kind; in the higher, by a stubborn and deliberate resistance, especially by a general agreement to import no merchandize from Great Britain until the stamp-act should be repealed. With the temper which prevailed from one end of the colonies to the other, and with the well known perseverance, bordering upon obstinacy, of the author of the project, perhaps this first struggle might have ended in the total separation, had not just at that time the administration in England fallen into other hands.

The ministry, which in the summer of 1765 took the affairs of the nation in hand, rejected the new system of immediate taxation in America entirely. The mild principles and the popular maxims of the marquis of Rockingham made him averse to a path in which violence alone could lead to the goal; and the secretary of state, general Conway, had been, when the business was first transacted in parliament, Grenville's most powerful and ardent opposer. The stamp-act, in the first session of the year 1766, was repealed; but to preserve the honour of parliament from sinking altogether, with this repeal was connected a declaratory act, intituled, "An Act for securing the Dependence of the Colonies"; in which the right of Great Britain to legislate for the colonies in all cases whatsoever was solemnly maintained.

This last step could not in itself be indifferent to the Americans; yet the joy at the repeal of the stamp-act was so great that no regard was paid to the possible consequences of the act, which was attached as a counterbalancing weight to this appeal; and probably peace and concord would have been for a long time restored and secured, had not the English ministry, in a luckless hour, brought again to light the fatal project of raising a revenue from America. The marquis of Rockingham's administration had been dissolved soon after the repeal of the stamp-act, and had been succeeded by another, at the head of which was indeed the name, but no longer the genius, of the earl of Chatham. Charles Townsend, chancellor of the exchequer, a man of splendid talents but of a frivolous and unsafe character, who was aiming to attain the highest summit of influence in the state when an early death snatched him away from the career, proposed, in the year 1767, a tax upon the importation of glass, paper, painters' colours and tea into the colonies, and this proposal, although several of the ministers, and among the rest the duke of Grafton, who was at the head of the treasury department, had silently contended against it, was by parliament adopted as a law. The defenders of this new plan entrenched themselves behind the feeble argument that although parliament, by repealing the stamp-act, had renounced a direct taxation of the colonies, yet no renunciation could thence be inferred of indirect taxation, which was intimately connected with the right of regulating trade.

Had this reasoning even silenced the opposition in parliament, it was by no means calculated to satisfy the colonies. The hostile object of the new statute could not escape the shortest sight. The taxes prescribed, being announced merely as impost duties, were indeed reconcileable with the letter of that immunity which lay so near the heart of the colonists, but their secret object could scarcely be any other than to wrest by artifice what was not ventured to be maintained by force. The insignificance of the benefit England could derive from these taxes, which would have produced only about £20,000, but too strongly confirmed this suspicion; and the peculiar character of the new regulations, the iniquity of exacting from a people, compelled to receive all the articles they needed exclusively from the mother country, a tax upon the importation of such articles, rendered the undertaking completely odious. The imposts of 1767 operated in exactly the same manner as the stamp-act; the general non-importation agreement was renewed in all the colonies; bitter controversies between the colonial assemblies and the royal governors, violent scenes between the citizens of divers towns and the military, resistance on the one part, menaces on the other, foreboded the stroke which was soon to shake the British empire to its foundations.

The ministry seemed however to make one more stand upon the very border of the precipice. In the year 1769, by a circular letter of the minister for the colonies, the pleasing prospect of a speedy relief from the odious impost duties was opened to the colonial assemblies, and the decided aversion of the duke of Grafton to the taxation of America seemed to encourage the hopes which this letter had raised. But no sooner had he, in the beginning of 1770, resigned his office than the affair took another turn. His successor, lord North, did indeed in the first days of his administration formally propose the repeal of the American imposts, but with the unfortunate exception that the tax upon tea should be continued as a proof of the legitimate authority of parliament; nor could the most vehement opposition of the united Rockingham and Grenville parties, who painted in the strongest colours the folly of continuing the contest after the benefit was abandoned, avail any thing against this wretched plan.[3] From that hour it was clear that the ministry had no other object than to make the colonies feel their chains. The first steps in this slippery career had their grounds in false representations and partial judgments; instead of these *errors* dangerous *passions* were now introduced, and the peace and welfare of the nation were to be sacrificed to a mistaken ambition and a destructive jealousy.

Meanwhile, the disposition to resistance had struck deep roots in

[3] Lord North formally declared in parliament that after what had happened an entire repeal of all the new taxes could not take place until America should be brought to the feet of Great Britain.

all the colonies; and the wider the mother country's undertakings departed from their first object, the more the resistance of the Americans departed from its original character. They had at first only denied the right of parliament to tax them; by degrees the sphere of their opposition extended, and they began to call in question the authority of parliament altogether. When they had once taken this ground, it was in vain to hope to drive them from it. The consciousness of their stability, and their distance from England, their lawful pride in the rights derived from their British descent, the recollection of the circumstances which had led their forefathers to America, the sight of the flourishing state into which in a period of 150 years they had turned an uninhabitable desert, the injustice and the harshness of those who, instead of alleviating their dependence by gentle treatment, were daily seeking to render it more oppressive;—all this encouraged the new impulse which their ideas and their wishes had taken. The folly of Great Britain in abandoning for the useless discussion of a problematic right the undisturbed enjoyment of a connection which, though never analysed and dissected with theoretic accuracy, was even in its undefined state so advantageous, became continually more visible; but far from endeavouring with tender caution to heal the dangerous wound, measure upon measure was taken to inflame it. Almost every step taken by the government during this unhappy period in respect to the internal administration of the colonies, to the courts of justice, to the provincial assemblies, to the relations between the civil and military authorities, seemed expressly calculated at once to embitter and to embolden discontent; and the spirit of insurrection had long been in full possession of every mind when a new attempt of the ministry made it suddenly burst forth with the utmost violence.

The persevering refusal of the Americans to import tea into the colonies, so long as the tax upon it prescribed in the year 1767 and purposely retained in 1770 should not be repealed, had occasioned a considerable loss to the East India company, in whose magazines great quantities of this article perished unconsumed. They had offered the minister to pay upon the exportation double the trifling tax of three pence upon the pound, which was yet so odious to the colonies; but this proposal, advantageous as it was, and which opened so honourable an issue from the crisis, was disapproved and rejected as not according with the system of reducing America to unconditional submission. But as the embarrassment of the company was continually growing greater, they sought to help themselves by another project and concluded to ship the tea for America upon their own account, there to pay the impost by their own agents and then make their sales. As at the same time, by act of parliament, the exportation was made duty free, whereby the tea, notwithstanding the impost in America, would be at a cheaper market than it had before been, it was hoped that the Americans would abandon all their scruples and, not feeling immediately the tax lurking in the price of the article, would give up all resistance.

The event soon discovered how vain this hope had been. Time had been allowed the colonies to reflect upon their situation, and to judge of the ministerial proceeding in the point of view which was alone essential. The merchants, who during the American agreement against the importation of British tea had enriched themselves by the contraband trade of foreign teas, might, perhaps, only from mercantile considerations, abhor the undertaking of the East India company sanctioned by the government; but the great mass of the people, and the most enlightened patriots in America, saw and condemned in this undertaking nothing but the evident purpose of carrying through the taxing right of the British parliament. The remarkable circumstance that England had refused the larger revenue which the taxes upon exportation from the British ports would have produced to secure the levying of the much smaller entrance duty in America betrayed a bitter passionate obstinacy which, together with so many other symptoms of hostility, threatened the colonies with a gloomy futurity.

When the first report of these tea-ships having been sent arrived in America, from Newhampshire to Georgia universal preparations for the most animated resistance were made. The agents of the company nowhere dared to receive the goods; in New York, Philadelphia, and many other towns such strong protestations against unlading the ships were made that they were compelled to return untouched. In Boston, where the spirit of resistance had been from the beginning the most violent, Governor Hutchinson adopted measures to make the return of the ships impossible before the object should be attained; but his rigor only served to increase the evil. A small number of decided opponents went on board the ship and, without doing any other damage, broke open 342 chests of tea and threw it into the sea.

The account of these tumultuous proceedings, soon after the opening of parliament in the year 1774, reached England where, immediately, the thirst for revenge silenced every other feeling; the zeal to maintain the honour and the rights of government [overcame] every other council, not only in the minds of the ministers, but likewise in the general opinion of the nation. In this critical moment it was forgotten that it was not until after the colonies for ten years long had been driven by a series of vicious and hazardous measures, by attacks continually repeated, and by studied systematic vexations to the utmost extremity, that their just indignation had burst forth in illegal acts.

The necessity for severe measures was indeed now evident, even to the moderate. But unfortunately, resentment overstepped the bounds of equity, and provoked pride the bounds of policy. The immediate authors of the excesses in Boston might justly have been punished; the East India company might justly claim to be indemnified by the colonies; the Americans, by their acts of violence, had evidently placed themselves at a disadvantage; and their faults gave the most favourable opportunity to bring them, with wisdom, back within their bounds. But England seemed herself to spurn all the advantages of her present situation, and to have commenced a war, rather against her own welfare and security, than against the opposition in the colonies. The first measure, proposed by lord North, was a law to close as long as the king should think necessary the port of Boston, and to transfer the custom-house of that flourishing and important commercial town to another place. Immediately after, appeared a second law, which struck still deeper at the vital principle of the colonies, which scarcely could be justified by the most exaggerated ideas of the parliament's authority, and which could not but unavoidably drive to despair men who had already been almost impelled to insurrection by an impost tax. This harsh law declared the province of Massachusetts Bay's charter void, and subjected this province, which by its wealth, its constitution hitherto, and the sentiments of its inhabitants, seemed to be more dangerous to the government than all the rest, to a new organization grounded on an absolute dependence upon the crown. At the same time, another act of parliament ordained that persons who during the tumults in America had committed offences against public officers, in every case where the governor should have reason to apprehend that they could have no impartial trial there, should be sent to England for trial; a statute which, according to British ideas, deserved the epithet of tyrannical. Finally, the minister brought into parliament a law giving to the province of Canada, which had been until then under a merely temporary administration, a constitution entirely different from the forms of the other colonial governments; and, however the most recent experience might seem to justify the government in this step, it could not but produce the most unfavourable operation in the colonies, who believed to read their own future destiny in the treatment of that neighbouring country.

As soon as these measures were known in America, the general indignation, irritated yet further by the reinforcement of the royal troops in Boston and by various unpleasant circumstances and oppressions inseparable from this event, was raised to the highest and most dangerous pitch. Instantaneously through all the colonies but one voice was heard: that the contest with England could be decided only by the sword. Preparations for the most resolute defence were everywhere the great occupation; exercises of arms became the sole employment of the citizens. A congress of fifty-one deputies from all the provinces assembled on the 4th of September, 1774, at Philadelphia, to consult upon the common grievances and upon the means of averting the common danger. The first measures of this assembly consisted in a solemn declaration that the unjust and oppressive proceeding of parliament against the town of Boston and the province of Massachusetts Bay, was to be considered as the cause of all the colonies; and in a recommendation to the inhabitants of North America to suspend all commercial intercourse with Great Britain until the just grievances of the colonies should be redressed. Hereupon, the congress resolved upon an address to the British nation and another to the king of England in which the distressed situation of North America was delineated with boldness and energy, but at the same time with evident moderation, and in a language which still deprecated a separation from the mother country as a very great evil.

It could no longer be concealed to the dullest eye that the contest with the colonies had assumed a new and formidable character and had spread to such an extent as threatened the whole British empire. Yet nothing is more certain than that at this decisive moment it still depended upon the parliament to finish it happily. No resolution less than that of a total repeal of all the laws promulgated since 1766 was commensurate with the greatness of the danger; but the thought that the immediate loss of America was at stake should have reconciled every mind to this only remaining mean of salvation. Unfortunately, the deep exasperation, the inflexible pride, the false ambition, all the angry passions which this cruel system had introduced and nourished, maintained now likewise their predominance; and a fatal error, the opinion that the victory over the colonies would be infallible and easy, entered into an unholy league with all those passions. The parliament, at the beginning of the year 1775, in a remarkable address to the king, declared that both houses, convinced that a formal rebellion had broken out in the province of Massachusetts Bay, would faithfully support him in every measure against rebellious subjects. Immediately afterwards, several laws of unmerciful severity, by which the colonies were deprived of all foreign commerce and, what was yet harder, even of that fishery upon the coasts of Newfoundland so highly essential to their subsistence, passed by great majorities. Some of the wisest and most venerable statesmen, lord Chatham,[4] lord Camden, lord Shel-

[4] This great man, who, faithful to the principles of antient policy, and animated with the most unbounded zeal for the glory and welfare of his country, which under his administration had reached the zenith of her greatness, considered the separation of the colonies from England as the greatest of all evils, said among other things, in a most impressive speech, with which on the 20th of January, 1775, he introduced the motion for withdrawing the troops from Boston: "I announce it to you now, my lords, we shall one day be *compelled* to repeal these oppressive regulations, they *must* be repealed; you yourselves will retract them. I pledge myself for it; I stake my reputation upon it; I am content to pass for a blockhead, if they are not retracted."

It is furthermore very remarkable that the disapprobation of the measures against America was not confined to the then *opposition parties,* but was equally shown by several of the principal ministers. The duke of Grafton, who from 1766 to 1770, was first lord of the treasury, and afterwards, from 1771 to 1775, keeper of the seals, had at all times declared himself against the prevailing system; the same sentiments were ascribed to the earl of Dartmouth, secretary of state for America; lord North himself, who from 1770, was considered as first minister, is said to have manifested often in the deliberations of the cabinet different principles from those he afterwards supported in parliament. But nothing can be more surprising than that in one of the most violent debates, which took

burne, in the upper house, Edmund Burke, colonel Barré, and others in the house of commons, exerted in vain against these desperate resolutions all the powers of an astonishing eloquence, such as perhaps had never been surpassed. The several plans of conciliation which they proposed were rejected, always with displeasure, sometimes with contempt; the only step towards peace that ever was attempted rested upon a project of lord North, evidently incompetent to the end, which would scarcely have satisfied the colonies at the outset of the dispute, and certainly could not content them in the year 1775.

The congress assembled for the second time in May, 1775, and declared, "that by the violation of the charter of Massachusetts Bay, the connection between that colony and the crown was dissolved." The conciliatory bills of lord North were rejected; a *continental army* and a *paper currency* were created; colonel Washington was appointed commander in chief of the American troops, &c. The war at this period had, in fact, broken out; it had been opened by the battle of Lexington, on the 19th of April, and while the congress were adopting these resolutions, a second and much bloodier action took place at Bunker's hill, where the loss suffered by the English army gave a severe, though unfortunately a fruitless, lesson to those who had treated with so much contempt the resistance and the military talents of the Americans.

Although every hope of peace had now well nigh vanished, the Congress were not however so far discouraged as to decline venturing, even at this period, a last attempt at conciliation. They resolved a second address to the king, in which the colonies under the most forcible assurances of their submission, and of their unabated wish to remain united with Great Britain, intreated in the most urgent manner, that his majesty would give his assent to any plan whatsoever, calculated to pacify this wretched contest. The address was presented on the 1st of September 1775, by Mr. Penn, of Pennsylvania, one of the most respectable citizens of North Amer-

---

place in the house of lords in February, 1775, even lord Mansfield, a man in high consideration, and of great talents, but whom the whig party considered as an exaggerated partizan of the crown's rights, and as one of the most decided enemies of the Americans, carried away by the heat of the contest, formally declared that the introduction of imposts in the year 1767 was the most *absurd* and most *pernicious* measure that could have been devised, and had been the real cause of all the subsequent misfortunes.

ica, who was informed "that no answer would be given to it." Soon after the minister brought into parliament the law which prohibited all intercourse with the colonies and declared their ships to be lawful prize; a law which was justly considered as a declaration of war against America, and by some as a formal abdication of the right of government over the colonies. At the same time, the king concluded alliances with several German princes, who engaged their troops for a great undertaking; and preparations of every kind announced that force alone was to decide the destiny of the British empire. At the close of the session of parliament in February, 1776, the bitterness had attained its highest pitch. Even the evident danger that foreign powers, and France in particular, might take a part in the disturbances in America and take advantage of England's embarrassment made no impression upon the ministers and the parliament. When some members of the opposition at the beginning of the year 1776 asserted that according to very authentic accounts, a negociation between the Congress at Philadelphia and the French court was already commenced, not only the truth, but even the possibility of this but too well grounded fact was denied. It was maintained "that such an unexampled fascination could not be supposed in any nation holding colonies itself, in any government wishing to retain the obedience of their own subjects." A reasoning, which in itself rested upon very just principles, but which lost all its conclusive *weight* in the mouth of those who, by a fascination entirely similar, had come to the point of setting at stake, from mere stupid obstinacy, one of their most precious possessions and half the existence of their empire.

Since the last months of the year 1775, the war was raging in the bowels of the colonies. The language and the resolves of Parliament in the winter of 1775-1776, taught the Americans that it would be a war for life and death. Every bond of union was broken. Against the return of the old happy days the iron hand of inexorable destiny had barred every gate. On the 4th of July 1776, the Congress declared the Independence of the Thirteen United States.

It belongs not to the purpose of the present essay to continue further this cursory historical recapitulation, since I am here speaking only of the *origin* of the American revolution. It is however sufficiently known that the *progress* and the *issue* of the war completely justified the anticipations of those who would have avoided it *at any price*. It is equally well known how much the *consequences* of this war have put to shame the expectations of all parties. The supporters of the war went upon the principle that every thing must be hazarded to maintain the possession of the colonies, its opponents upon the principle that every thing must be *sacrificed* not to lose them; both concurred therefore in the opinion that this loss would give a deep and perhaps incurable wound to the British empire. Experience has decided. In a few years after the loss of the colonies England has again become as powerful and flourishing, nay more powerful and flourishing than ever. And whatever of a hurtful nature that lay in the influence of this event upon the affairs of Europe has fallen upon *France* alone; upon France who, according to the general opinion, was to derive the greatest advantages from the American revolution.

If we duly meditate upon the series of facts which have been here summarily exhibited, and upon some others equally certain and authentic which will be touched upon in the sequel, the following points of comparison will arise to show in its clearest light the *essential* difference between the American and French revolutions.

The American revolution was grounded partly upon principles of which the right *was evident*, partly upon such as it was at least very questionable whether they were not right, and from beginning to end upon no one that was clearly and decidedly wrong; the French revolution was an uninterrupted series of steps, the wrong of which could not, upon rigorous principles, for a moment be doubted.

The question concerning the *right* of a revolution has, by the frivolous way of thinking, by the shallow sophistry, and even by the immense devastations—and the stupid indifference arisen from them—of this revolutionary age, been in a manner discarded among the idle amusements of scholastic pedants; many who hold themselves for statesmen think it no longer *worth while so much as* to start the question; yet in the eyes of the thinking, of the wise and the good, will it ever remain the first and the last.

The relation between the inhabitants of a distant colony and the government of the mother country is never to be compared in all respects with the relation between the government and their immediate subjects. In the former, there lies always something strained, something equivocal, something unnatural; for it cannot be denied, the firmest foundation of all sovereignty is in the wants of the governed, and those wants are weaker, are more questionable, withdraw themselves, to express myself so, from the eyes and the feeling, when the government is a thousand leagues distant from the country which must obey their laws. Besides, all the European states which founded or encouraged the foundation of colonies in the other quarters of the globe, considered these colonies, more or less, as mere instruments to *enrich* and strengthen the seat of their own power, and treated the people who inhabited them merely as the means of an happier or more agreeable existence for their own [people]. A maxim, which could not easily be reconciled with the general purposes of society, for which the colonies must have as keen a sense as the mother country, and with the consciousness of independent stability, to which they must sooner or later attain. Hence, the right of an European nation over their colonies must necessarily always be a wavering, insecure, undefined, and often undefinable right. If, however, the form of government in the mother country be simple, and the conditions upon which the colony was founded were in themselves clear and definite, then that unavoidable misrelation will be less perceptible. The difficulties on the other hand must be much greater, the collisions more frequent and momentous, when the mother country has a complicated constitution, and when the conditions under which the colonies are connected with her, the rights which they enjoy by virtue of her particular constitution, the place which they are to hold in that constitution, are not in the precisest manner defined at their very origin.

This was in both points the case with the English colonies in North America. How far the rights and liberties of a new state, founded by Britons under the British constitution, should extend, and in what particular relation the inhabitants of such a state should stand with the several component parts of that mixed constitution? this was a question which at their [i.e., its] origin should have been considered with the utmost attention. This question was never once thought of. The colonies originated at a time when the British constitution itself had not yet attained its last perfection and consistence.[5] Their charters all proceeded from the *crown*. The parliament had never taken any part in their settlement.

The internal forms of government of these colonies were as various as the circumstances under which they had been founded or formed. Some of the most important had been granted as hereditary property to private persons, so that these and their heirs might govern them entirely as they pleased, and were scarcely more than under a nominal dependence upon the crown. In this manner had Maryland been granted to lord Baltimore; North and South Carolina to lord Clarendon; in this manner Pennsylvania and Delaware belonged to the family of the celebrated Penn. Others, as New Hampshire, New York, New Jersey, and Virginia were called royal provinces, and in these the king was considered as the immediate sovereign. Lastly, there was a third class of colonies, which were called privileged, and in which the power of the monarch was limited by the original charters. Such was the constitution of Massachusetts, of Rhode Island, and of Connecticut.

The relations between the royal governors and the provincial assemblies were in every colony differently defined and modified; but the provoncial assemblies were accustomed every where, whether the province was originally privileged, royal, or hereditary, more or less to exercise the right of enacting laws for the internal police of the province, of levying taxes for meeting the public exigences of the state, and of taking an essential part in every thing belonging to the administration of the country. In no single colony, however its constitution in respect to its dependance upon the crown was organized, was there a trace of a constitutional and legal authority vested in the British parliament. The charters contained none; no definite law, not so much as a partial statute, enacted in Great Britain, had ever proclaimed or even made mention of such an authority.

In the beginning, the parliament considered this their absolute exclusion from the sovereignty over the colonies with great indifference; in the preceding century the bounds of their power in

[5] Most of the colonies were founded before the middle of the seventeenth century; all before the revolution of 1688. The province of Georgia, the most southern of the colonies, and which was originally part of South Carolina, was the only one which received her *separate* constitution since the beginning of this century (in 1732), and was likewise the only one for the settlement and cultivation of which the British government had been at any cost.

general were so little defined that not the smallest doubt has been started against the authority of the king at his pleasure to give, to grant, to constitute, to privilege, to govern by himself, or allow to be governed by others, an immense continent in America; this distant and uncultivated land was besides far too much despised for them to concern themselves about its constitution. But when, on the one side, after the revolution of 1688, the influence of parliament upon all the affairs of government had become greater, firmer, and more general; and when, on the other side, the extraordinary importance of the colonies in their rapidly growing population, in their constantly improving culture, in their unexpected and splendid flourishing state, was daily more evident, the idea by degrees crept into every mind that so great and essential a part of the British empire could not possibly be altogether withdrawn from the superintendency of parliament, even though nothing should have been said of it hitherto in the public transactions.

In one single though truly important point, the parliament had always exercised the legislative power over the colonies, in every thing which concerned trade, whether of export or of import. Although this was precisely the seat of that mighty monopoly which seemed to give the colonies their whole value, and which, on the other side, could never be so favourable to their progress as liberty would have been, yet they willingly submitted to the regulations and restraints of all kinds with which the parliament in ample measure provided them. It appeared natural and equitable to themselves that the supreme legislative power in the empire should regulate and direct a concern which interested not exclusively America, but England too, in a much higher degree. The right of the parliament, therefore, to prescribe laws to the colonies relating to commerce, and to every thing connected with it, was never called in question.

But, as soon as the parliament determined to overstep this right and to levy taxes in America without the consent of the local representatives, the most vehement resistance could not fail to break out, and this resistance could as little fail to increase when, in the progress of the contest, the pretention to bind America by act of parliament, in all cases whatsoever, was advanced and formally derived from what was called the legal supremacy of parliament. The *omnipotence* of parliament, so often and so loudly then resounded by the antagonists of the colonies, was a very just principle for England, but a very invalid one for America. With the parliament, bating the trade laws to which the colonists submitted from reason and necessity, America had not the least to do. America sent no representatives to parliament, nor did it ever occur to parliament to offer her that power, which would indeed not have been without great difficulties carried into effect. The colonies, nevertheless, possessed all the benefits of the British constitution and even the greatest part of their forms. Almost in every one of them there was a *representative assembly,* which supplied the place of a lower house, and a senate, which answered to the house of peers. These assemblies transacted, under the sanction of the monarch, all the affairs which in England and Ireland were done by the parliaments. They enacted laws, levied taxes, deliberated upon the exigencies and upon the administration of their provinces. They formed, in concurrence with the king and his governors, a complete government organized altogether in the spirit of the English constitution, and needed no co-operation of the British parliament. The constitutions of the several provinces knew only the king and the provincial representative bodies, and had no more reference to the parliament of Great Britain than to the parliaments of France. They had existed more than a century without knowing any thing of the English parliament, otherwise than by its commercial regulations, which had not always been to them the most agreeable. The pretended right of parliament to prescribe laws and taxes for them was an arbitrary assumption against which the colonies, according to all legal principles, might proceed exactly as Great Britain would have done, had any of the provincial assemblies undertaken, with the concurrence of the king, to levy taxes in England or Scotland, or to overthrow the municipal constitution of London or Westminster, as the parliament had overthrown the charter of Massachusetts Bay.

The resistance of the colonies and the unavoidable insurrection which was finally produced by the continuance of the attack were, therefore, inasmuch as they respected the parliament, perfectly *right.* The parliament was, in regard to the colonies, to be considered as a *foreign power.* So long as this power had remained within the bounds of its silently acknowledged sphere of operation, the colonies had submitted to it. To give laws beyond those bounds, it was as little authorised as would have been the legislative power of any other nation. The Americans could resist it with the same right as they might have resisted the States-General of Holland, or the council of the Indies in Madrid, had these undertaken to impose upon them their manufacturing regulations or stamp taxes.

The question seems to be more difficult, with what right the colonies could likewise resist the king, who, at any rate, was their legal and acknowledged sovereign? But, if in this respect the lawfulness of their conduct be doubtful, it would at least remain a great point that its unlawfulness could not be clearly proved, and a closer examination will lead us to a result yet far more favourable to the justification of this conduct.

For there is a very evident distinction between an insurrection in a *simple,* and one in a *complicated,* or *mixed constitution.* In a simple government, every resistance against the supreme power is absolutely illegal and requires no further examination to be condemned. In a mixed government, cases may be imagined in which the matter is very intricate, and therefore problematic and dubious.

In a mixed government, the supreme power, or the proper sovereign, consists always of several component parts connected together and regulated by the constitution. Each of these parts has its constitutional rights and prerogatives; and those of any one part, though in themselves more important, cannot be more sacred than those of any other. When either of them exceeds its legal bounds and oppresses or endeavours to destroy another, this latter, unless the constitution be an empty name, must have the right of resisting; and, unless the war arising from this resistance be not averted by some fortunate expedient; if the old balance cannot again be restored, the contest must necessarily and *legally* end with the dissolution of the constitution. For between two independent component parts of the supreme power in a state, there can no more be a judge than between two independent states. That this is a most unfortunate situation for the whole nation interested in it, is self evident. The most dreadful circumstance it brings with it is unquestionably this, that the people in such a controversy never know whom to obey and whom to resist; for whom to declare, and against whom to act; that all rights and duties are thrown into confusion and involved in obscurity, and that it becomes a problem, who is within, and who is without the line of insurrection. This evil is inseparable from mixed forms of government;[6] and however great it may be, its possibility can never be excluded from such constitutions. If, for example, the two houses of the British parliament should make the attempt to enact laws without the sanction of the king, or the king without the concurrence of parliament, the injured party would beyond all doubt resist, and resist with energy; nor could any one deny that this resistance, even though it should end in civil war and the ruin of the constitution, was perfectly lawful.

The American colonies were precisely in this, or at least in an extremely similar situation. Their constitution before the revolution was evidently a monarchy, more or less limited by the influence of their provincial assemblies. The legislative and executive powers were divided between the king and the provincial assemblies, as in England, between the king and the two houses of parliament. The king and his governor had only a negative [veto] upon acts of legislation, and the provincial assemblies in most of the colonies had a considerable share in the government. In all the provinces (Pennsylvania since 1700 excepted) these assemblies were divided into two houses, closely corresponding in their functions with the two branches of the British parliament. The lower house, or the representative assembly, possessed everywhere the exclusive right of prescribing taxes. In some colonies, for instance in Maryland, the king, by the charter, *had expressly* renounced all right of taxation. In several others he had, in the literal sense of the word, only reserved the empty title of sovereignty. Connecticut and Rhode Island were perfect democracies. The colonial assemblies of these provinces chose their governors without the confirmation of the king and dismissed them at pleasure; they allowed no appeals from their courts of justice; their laws required no royal assent; nay,

[6] This is undoubtedly the greatest failing that can be objected against mixed governments. Fortunately, however, it must be acknowledged that the probability of such a dissolution is more remote in proportion as the constitution approaches nearer to perfection. For the more easily one of the constituted authorities can resist the other by its appropriate weight, the less will be the necessity of appealing to arms. On the other hand, the more imperfect the balance is, the greater will be the danger of a civil war. In this lies properly the decided superiority of the British constitution above all other complicated forms of government that ever were, or probably ever will be devised.

what is more remarkable, and a proof of their absolute independence, their charters granted them even the right of peace and war.

The king's power was, therefore, in all the colonies, more or less limited; in some to such a degree that it could not be compared with his legitimate power in Great Britain; and the colonial assemblies had a constitutional right to resist him when he violated their constitutional powers. Now, the measures of the ministry from 1764 were evident attacks upon those powers. Whether the parliament had advised or confirmed those attacks was, as we have before shewn, nothing to the colonies; they had to do only with the king, and the king, according to their constitutions, could levy no taxes but such as the provincial assemblies proposed. The stamp-act of 1764 was, therefore, a violation of their rights; the impost act of 1767 was a violation of their rights; the act of 1770 which maintained the tea-tax to support the supremacy of parliament was a gross, and what was worst of all an insulting, violation of their rights. To punish them for their constitutional resistance against these unconstitutional resolves was a revolting injustice; the mode of punishment (the Boston port-bill, the bill to abolish the Massachusetts charter, &c.) was not merely a violation, it was an entire dissolution of their rights. It was nothing more than the proclamation of a *fact* when the congress, in 1775, declared, "that by the abolition of the Massachusetts charter, *the connection between that province and the crown was dissolved.*" No resource was left but that of repelling force by force. The convocation of their first congress was in itself not an illegal measure. This congress exercised originally only the same rights which were unquestionably within the powers of every provincial assembly. It represented a legal resistance, and sought the means of preserving to America the constitution she had hitherto possessed. It was not until after the ministry had spurned at peace, rejected every proposal of conciliation, and finally required unconditional submission, that is, had *dissolved the constitution,* that the congress proceeded to the declaration which substituted a new government in the stead of that which was destroyed.

Had the colonies had the design (and it cannot be denied that they manifested it clearly enough) in this whole contest to separate the king completely from the parliament, all the means were taken away from them of regulating their conduct according to a system founded upon such a separation. The most intimate union subsisted between the ministry and the parliament; nor was it possible to resist the one without quarrelling with the other. The king confirmed the hostile acts of parliament; he ceased to be the constitutional monarch of the colonies and entered into an alliance with those whom they considered as usurpers in a legal point of view. Had the king of England allied himself with a foreign power (and in a constitutional sense the parliament was no other to the colonies) against the parliament of Great Britain, how would it be possible for the parliament to arm against this foreign power and yet spare the king of England? Or rather, would not the mere undertaking of such an alliance include within itself an immediate justification of every defensive measure taken by the injured party and an absolute renunciation of the constitution.

I think I have here sufficiently developed the first point in the comparison I proposed, that which relates to the conduct of North America; there now remains only the easy task of exhibiting the second, which relates to the conduct of France.

The single period of the disturbances in France, when mention was made of militating *rights,* was that in which the parliaments took part, in 1787 and 1788. If the prerogatives of these parliaments were not so great and so unquestionable as they would have represented them, yet their appeal to them gave at least a colour of lawfulness to their undertakings. That period, however, is to be considered only as preparatory to the real revolution.

From the breaking out of this revolution, the question as to the *lawfulness* of what the popular leaders did was never (an extraordinary, yet an indubitable fact!) started. The word *right* would have vanished from the French language had not an imaginary right of the *nation* to do whatever they, or their representatives should please, appeared as a sort of substitute for all other rights.

This is not the place to analyse this *right of the nation,* sometimes likewise called *right of man,* a sort of magic spell, with which all the ties of nations and of humanity were insensibly dissolved. Those who were serious in advancing [this right] grounded it upon the chimerical principle of the sovereignty of the people, which I have endeavoured upon another occasion to elucidate. Thus much is certain, that the leaders of the revolution, under the shelter of this talisman, spared themselves and others the trouble of enquiring into the lawfulness of their proceedings; for in their system all was right which they resolved upon in the name of the *people,* or in the name of mankind.

In order to judge of their actions according to their deserts, they must be snatched away from the tribunal they have erected for themselves and placed at another bar, whose laws accord better with the dictates of uncorrupted reason, and the eternal prescriptions of *real right.*

When the deputies of the states [estates], assembled together in the year 1789 they had beyond all doubt the *right* to undertake great reforms in the government, and even in the constitution of the French monarchy. This right, however, they could exercise only under the three following conditions. First, that they should observe the general forms of an assembly of the states in France until these forms should in a *lawful* manner be abolished or changed. Secondly, that their laws should not have the force of laws until assented to by the monarch. And thirdly, that they should follow the instructions given them by their constituents.

In less than six weeks they had broken through these three fundamental conditions. The deputies of the third state, without the least authority, and with a shameful violation of the rights of the other states, declared that themselves alone constituted the national assembly.

When the king endeavoured to bring them back from this monstrous usurpation to their proper limits, they declared to him that they persisted in it, formally renounced obedience to him, and reduced him finally to the necessity of commanding the two other estates to acknowledge the usurpation.

That in the immeasurable career which these two first successful acts of violence had opened they might no longer meet resistance from any quarter, they declared that the instructions of their constituents were not binding upon them.

They had proceeded thus far when, partly by their influence and example, partly by faults of the court, which need not be considered here, where the question only relates to *right,* the general rebellion broke out in Paris and in all the provinces. Far from *disapproving* this rebellion which, in perfect contrast with the rising of the people in America, had not the most distant connection with the lawful objects of the national assembly, they cherished and fostered it, gave it legislative force and consistence, conferred civic crowns upon its authors, called it an holy and virtuous insurrection, and took care to have it maintained in a continual flame during the whole period of their government.

Under the shadow of this insurrection they, who had placed themselves at its head, and taken upon themselves all responsibility, in a period of two years ran through the most remarkable circle of violation of all rights, public and private, that the world ever beheld. They drew up, without ever so much as *asking the free assent of the king,* a constitution so called, the incompetency, the impracticability, the ridiculous absurdity of which was so great that, even among its authors—(another unexampled yet undubitable fact) not a single man would ever have seriously defended it. This constitution they compelled the king, upon pain of being immediately dethroned, to subscribe and swear to.

Scarcely had this happened when their successors, who by virtue of this constitution alone had a sort of legal existence, and held something resembling an authority to shew, instead of governing and quieting the state according to this constitution, directed all their secret, and what was still more revolting, all their public measures to its destruction. In less than a year they succeeded in effecting this new usurpation. Without so much as having a *legal pretext,* they suspended the constitution, dethroned the king, assumed to themselves, still forsooth *in the name of the people,* the power of calling a *national convention,* and proclaimed the republic, with fewer formalities than a man would use to change his dress. By long habit dead to every sentiment of *right,* tormented by all the furies, plunged by their frantic measures, by crimes, and calamities of every kind into the lowest depth of criminal fool-hardiness, they now proclaimed against humanity and all its rights a formal, irreconcileable war; and to shut behind them every door for return, and to snap the last thread by which they still held together with a lawful existence, they finally murdered justice herself, in the person of the most conscientious and upright monarch who had ever adorned a throne.

The French revolution, therefore, began by a violation of rights, every step of its progress was a violation of rights, and it was never easy until it had succeeded to establish absolute wrong as the supreme and acknowledged maxim of a state completely dissolved, and yet existing only in bloody ruins.

3.

GEORGE BANCROFT

George Bancroft (1800-1891) was the most learned historian of the Revolution in his generation and perhaps in any generation. He was also an ardent supporter of Jacksonian democracy, Secretary of the Navy under Polk, minister to Great Britain (1846-49) and to Prussia (1867-74). Writing before most of the papers of the period had been collected, sorted, edited, or published, he nevertheless gained access to a vast number of historical documents, public and private, that have since become more readily available to scholars in historical societies, archives, and libraries. Drawing heavily on these original sources, Bancroft created an epic story of the Revolution as a struggle for human freedom and popular government. He never condensed his interpretation to the form of an essay, but neither did he ever leave his readers in doubt about the significance of the events he described.

The passages that follow are from a volume that carried on each page the running head: "How Britain Estranged America." The first two passages contain some of Bancroft's comments on the British Parliament and on George III. The final passage is his chapter describing the enactment of the "Intolerable Acts" of 1774. All three are from his final revision, published in 1890, which was a condensation of his first, somewhat longer, version published in 1854. (Reprinted from George Bancroft, History of the United States of America from the Discovery of the Continent, *The Au-*

thor's Last Revision. Six volumes, New York, 1890, Volume III, pp. 280-83, 382-83, 466-82.)

[On the British government in 1768, to which the customs officers in Boston had appealed for military assistance]

To insure the arrival of an armed force, the commissioners of the customs applied directly to the naval commander at Halifax, and sent a second memorial to the lords of the treasury. They said that a design had certainly been formed to bring them, on the eighteenth of March, to Liberty Tree, and oblige them to renounce their commissions. "The governor and magistracy," they add, "have not the least authority or power in this place. We depend on the favor of the mob for our protection. We cannot answer for our security for a day, much less will it be in our power to carry the revenue laws into effect."

These letters went from Boston to the ministry in March. The tales of riots were false. The people were opposed to the revenue system of the British parliament, and hoped for redress; if the ministry should refuse it, they were resolved to avoid every act of violence, to escape paying the taxes, and to induce their repeal by never buying the goods on which they were imposed. England had on her side the general affection of the people, the certainty that the country could not as yet manufacture for itself, and the consequent certainty that schemes of non-importation would fail. Would she but substitute a frank and upright man for Bernard [Francis Bernard, governor of Massachusetts 1760-69], the wants of the colonists might weary them of their self-denial.

But the administration of public affairs had degenerated into a system of patronage which had money for its object; and was supported by the king, from the love of authority. The government of England had more and more ceased to represent the noble spirit of England. The twelfth parliament, which had taxed America and was now near its dissolution, exceeded all former ones in profligacy. Direct gifts of money were grown less frequent, as public opinion increased in power; but there never was a parliament so shameless in its corruption as this twelfth parliament, which virtually severed America from England. It had its votes ready for the minister of any party. It gave an almost unanimous support to Pitt, when, for the last time in seventy years, the foreign politics of England were on the side of liberty. It had a majority for Newcastle after he had ejected Pitt; for Bute, when he dismissed Newcastle; for Grenville, so long as he was the friend of Bute; for Grenville, when he became Bute's implacable foe; and for the inexperienced Rockingham. When Charles Townshend, rebelling in the cabinet, seemed likely to become minister, he commanded its applause. When Townshend died, North easily restored subordination.

Nor was it more scrupulous as to any measure which the minister of the hour might propose. It promoted the alliance with the king of Prussia, and deserted him; it protected the issue of general warrants, and utterly condemned them; it passed the stamp act, and repealed the stamp act; it began to treat America with tenderness, then veered about, imposed new taxes, changed American constitutions, and trifled with the freedom of the American legislative. It was corrupt, and knew itself to be corrupt, and made a jest of its corruption; and when it was gone, and had no more chances at prostitution, men wrote its epitaph as of the most scandalously abandoned body that England had ever known.

Up to a recent time, the colonists had looked to parliament as the bulwark of their liberties; henceforward, they knew it to be their most dangerous enemy. They avowed that they would not pay taxes which it assumed to impose. Some still allowed it a right to restrain colonial trade, but the advanced opinion among the patriots was that each provincial legislature must be perfectly free; that laws were not valid unless sanctioned by the consent of America herself. Without disputing what the past had established, they were resolved to oppose any minister that should attempt to "innovate" a single iota in their privileges. "Almighty God himself," wrote Dickinson, "will look down upon your righteous contest with approbation. You will be a band of brothers, strengthened with inconceivable supplies of force and constancy by that sympathetic ardor which animates good men, confederated in a good cause. You are assigned by Divine Providence, in the appointed order of things, the protector of unborn ages, whose fate depends upon your virtue."

The men of Boston, whose fathers came to the wilderness for freedom to say their prayers, would not fear to take up arms against a preamble which implied their servitude. At a town-meeting, in March 1768, Malcolm moved their thanks to the ingenious author of the Farmer's Letters [John Dickinson, of Pennsylvania]; and Hancock, Samuel Adams, and Warren were of the committee to greet him in the name of the town as "the friend of Americans and the benefactor of mankind."

"They may with equal reason make one step more," wrote Hutchinson to the duke of Grafton: "they may deny the regal as well as the parliamentary authority, although no man as yet has that in his thoughts."

Du Châtelet [the French Ambassador], in England, having made his inquiries into the resources of America, was persuaded that, even if the detailed statements before him were one half too large, England could not reduce her colonies, should they raise the standard of rebellion. "Their population is so great," said he to Choiseul [the French foreign minister], "that a breath would scatter the troops sent to enforce obedience. The ever-existing attractions of an entire independence and of a free commerce cannot fail to keep their minds continually in a state of disgust at the national subjection. The English government may take some false step, which will in a single day set all these springs in activity. A great number of chances can hasten the revolution which all the world foresees without daring to assign its epoch. I please myself with the thought that it is not so far off as some imagine, and that we should spare neither pains nor expense to cooperate with it. We must nourish his Catholic majesty's disposition to avenge his wrongs. The ties that bind America to England are three-fourths broken. It must soon throw off the yoke. To make themselves independent, the inhabitants want nothing but arms, courage, and a chief. If they had among them a genius equal to Cromwell, this republic would be more easy to establish than the one of which that usurper was the head. Perhaps this man exists; perhaps nothing is wanting but happy circumstances to place him upon an exalted theatre."

At Mount Vernon, conversation with Arthur Lee fell on the

dangers that overhung the country. "Whenever my country calls upon me," said Washington, "I am ready to take my musket on my shoulder."

"Courage, Americans!" So, in April 1768, said William Livingston, one of the famed New York "triumvirate" of antiprelatic lawyers, through the press. "Liberty, religion, and sciences are on the wing to these shores. The finger of God points out a mighty empire to your sons. The land we possess is the gift of heaven to our fathers, and Divine Providence seems to have decreed it to our latest posterity. The day dawns in which the foundation of this mighty empire is to be laid, by the establishment of a regular American constitution. All that has hitherto been done seems to be little beside the collection of materials for this glorious fabric. 'Tis time to put them together. The transfer of the European part of the family is so vast, and our growth so swift, that, BEFORE SEVEN YEARS ROLL OVER OUR HEADS, the first stone must be laid."

[On George III, after the British decision in 1770 to retain the tax on tea imported into the colonies]

The decision came from the king, who was the soul of the ministry, busying himself even with the details of affairs. He had many qualities that become a sovereign: temperance, regularity, and industry; decorous manners and unaffected piety; frugality in his personal expenses, so that his pleasures laid no burden on his people; a moderation which made him averse to wars of conquest; courage, which dared to assume responsibility, and could even contemplate death serenely; a fortitude that rose with adversity.

But he was bigoted, morbidly impatient of being ruled, and incapable of reconciling the need of reform with the establishments of the past. He was the great founder and head of the new tory or conservative party, which had become dominant through his support. In zeal for authority, hatred of reform, and antipathy to philosophical freedom and to popular power, he was inflexibly obstinate and undisguised; nor could he be justly censured for dissimulation, except for that disingenuousness which studies the secret characters of men, in order to use them as its instruments. No one could tell whether the king really liked him. He could flatter, cajole, and humor, or frown and threaten; he could conceal the sense of injuries and forget good service; bribe the corrupt by favors, or terrify deserters by punishment. In bestowing rewards, it was his rule to make none but revocable grants; and he required of his friends an implicit obedience. He was willing to govern through parliament, yet was ready to stand by his ministers, even in a minority; and he was sure that one day the government must disregard majorities.

With a strong physical frame, he had a nervous susceptibility which made him rapid in his utterance; and so impatient of contradiction that he never could bear the presence of a minister who resolutely differed from him, and was easily thrown into a state of excitement bordering upon madness. Anger, which changed Chatham into a seer, pouring floods of light upon his mind and quickening his discernment, served only to cloud the mind of George III., so that he could not hide his thoughts from those about him, and, if using the pen, could neither spell correctly nor write coherently. Hence the proud, unbending Grenville was his aversion; and his years with the compliant Lord North, though full of public disasters, were the happiest of his life. Conscious of his devotion to the cause of legitimate authority, and viewing with complacency his own correctness of morals, he identified himself with the cause which he venerated. The crown was to him the emblem of all rightful power. He had that worst quality of evil, that he, as it were, adored himself; and regarded opposition to his designs as an offence against integrity and patriotism. He thought no exertions too great to crush the spirit of revolution, and no punishment too cruel or too severe for rebels.

[England reacts to the news of the Boston Tea Party]

The Crisis: February–May 1774

The ministry, overruling the lingering scruples of Dartmouth [Secretary of State for the Colonies], and Lord North [First Lord of the Treasury] decided that there existed a rebellion which required coercion. Inquiries were made, with the object of enabling the king to proceed in "England against the ringleaders," and inflict on them immediate and exemplary punishment. But, after laborious examinations before the privy council, and the close attention of Thurlow [attorney-general] and Wedderburn [solicitor-general], it appeared that British law and the British constitution set bounds to the anger of the government, which gave the first evidence of its weakness by acknowledging a want of power to wreak its will.

During the delay attending an appeal to parliament, the secretary of state would speak with the French minister of nothing but harmony; and he said to the representative of Spain: "Never was the union between Versailles, Madrid, and London so solid; I see nothing that can shake it." Yet the old distrust lurked under the pretended confidence.

One day in February 1774, while the government feared no formidable opposition, Charles James Fox, then of the treasury board, censured Lord North for want of decision and courage. "Greatly incensed at his presumption," the king wrote: "That young man has so thoroughly cast off every principle of common honor and honesty that he must become as contemptible as he is odious." Dismissed from office, and connected with no party, he was left free to follow his own generous impulses, and "to discover powers for regular debate, which neither his friends had hoped nor his enemies foreboded." Disinterested observers already predicted that he would one day be classed among the greatest statesmen of his country.

The cause of liberty obtained in him a friend who was independent of party allegiance and traditions, just when the passion for ruling America by the central authority was producing anarchy in the colonies. In South Carolina, whose sons esteemed themselves disfranchised on their own soil by the appointment of strangers to every office, the governor had for four years negatived every tax bill, in the hope of controlling the appropriations. In North Carolina the law establishing courts of justice had expired; in the conflict of claims of power between the governor and the legislature every new law on the subject was negatived, and there were no courts of any kind in the province. The most orderly and the best governed part of Carolina was the self-organized republic of Watauga, beyond the mountains, where the settlements were extending along the Holston, as well as south of the Nollichucky.

An intrepid population, heedless of proclamations, was pouring westward through all the gates of the Alleghanies; seating themselves on the New River and the Greenbrier, on the branches of the Monongahela, or even making their way to the Mississippi; accepting from nature their title-deeds to the unoccupied wilderness. Connecticut kept in mind that its charter bounded its territory by the Pacific; and had already taken courage to claim lands westward to the Mississippi, "seven or eight hundred miles in extent of the finest country and happiest climate on the globe. In fifty years," said they, pleasing themselves with visions of the happiness of their posterity and "the glory of this New World," "our people will be more than half over this tract, extensive as it is; in less than one century the whole may become even well cultivated. If the coming period bears due proportion to that from the first landing of poor distressed fugitives at Plymouth, nothing that we can in the utmost stretch of imagination fancy of the state of this country at an equally future period, can exceed what it will then be. A commerce will and must arise, independent of everything external, and superior to anything ever known in Europe, or of which a European can have an adequate idea." The commerce of Philadelphia and New York had outgrown the laws of trade; and the revenue officers, weary of attempts to enforce them, received what duties were paid almost as a favor.

The New England people who dwelt on each side of the Green Mountains repelled the jurisdiction which the royal government of

New York would have enforced even at the risk of bloodshed, and administered their own affairs by means of permanent committees.

The people of Massachusetts knew that "they had passed the river and cut away the bridge." In March, voting the judges of the superior court ample salaries from the colonial treasury, they called upon them to refuse the corrupting donative from the crown. Four of them yielded; Oliver, the chief justice, alone refused; the house, therefore, impeached him before the council, and declared him suspended till the issue of the impeachment. They began to familiarize the public mind to the thought of armed resistance, by ordering some small purchases of powder on account of the colony to be stored in a building of its own, and by directing the purchase of twelve pieces of cannon. "Don't put off the boat till you know where you will land," advised the timid. "We must put off the boat," cried Boston patriots, "even though we do not know where we shall land." "Put off the boat; God will bring us into a safe harbor," said Hawley of Northampton. "Anarchy itself," repeated one to another, "is better than tyranny."

The proposal for a general congress was deferred to the next June; but the committees of correspondence were to prepare the way for it. A circular letter explained why Massachusetts had been under the necessity of proceeding so far of itself, and entreated for its future guidance the benefit of the councils of the whole country. Hancock, on the fifth of March, spoke to a crowded audience in Boston: "Permit me to suggest a general congress of deputies from the several houses of assembly on the continent as the most effectual method of establishing a union for the security of our rights and liberties." "Remember," he continued, "from whom you sprang. Not only pray, but act; if necessary, fight, and even die, for the prosperity of our Jerusalem;" and, as he pointed out Samuel Adams, the vast multitude seemed to promise that in all succeeding times the great patriot's name, and with him "the roll of fellow-patriots, should grace the annals of history."

Samuel Adams prepared the last instructions of Massachusetts to Franklin. "It will be in vain," such were his solemn words officially pronounced, "for any to expect that the people of this country will now be contented with a partial and temporary relief; or that they will be amused by court promises, while they see not the least relaxation of grievances. By means of a brisk correspondence among the several towns in this province they have wonderfully animated and enlightened each other. They are united in sentiments, and their opposition to unconstitutional measures of government is become systematical. Colony begins to communicate freely with colony. There is a common affection among them; and shortly the whole continent will be as united in sentiment and in their measures of opposition to tyranny as the inhabitants of this province. Their old good-will and affection for the parent country are not totally lost; if she returns to her former moderation and good humor, their affection will revive. They wish for nothing more than a permanent union with her upon the condition of equal liberty. This is all they have been contending for; and nothing short of this will or ought to satisfy them."

Such was the ultimatum of America, sent by one illustrious son of Boston for the guidance of another. But the sense of the English people was manifestly with the ministers, who were persuaded that there was no middle way, and that the American continent would not interpose to shield Boston from the necessity of submission.

On the seventh of March, Dartmouth and North, grievously lamenting their want of greater executive power, and the consequent necessity of laying their measures before parliament, presented to the two houses a message from the king. "Nothing," said Lord North, "can be done to re-establish peace without additional powers." "The question now brought to issue," said Rice, on moving the address which was to pledge parliament to the exertion of every means in its power, "is whether the colonies are or are not the colonies of Great Britain." Nugent, now Lord Clare, entreated that there might be no divided counsels. "On the repeal of the stamp act," said Dowdeswell, "all America was quiet; but in the following year you would go in pursuit of a pepper-corn; you would collect from pepper-corn to pepper-corn; you would establish taxes as tests of obedience. Unravel the whole conduct of America; you will find out the fault is at home." "The dependence of the colonies is a part of the constitution," said Pownall, the former governor of Massachusetts. "I hope, for the sake of this country, for the sake of America, for the sake of general liberty, that this address will go with a unanimous vote."

Edmund Burke only taunted the ministry with their wavering policy. Lord George Germain derived all the American disturbance from the repeal of the stamp-tax. Conway pleaded for unanimity. "I speak," said William Burke, "as an Englishman; we applaud ourselves for the struggle we have had for our constitution; the colonists are our fellow-subjects; they will not lose theirs without a struggle." Barré thought the subject had been discussed with good temper, and refused to make any opposition. "The leading question," said Wedderburn, who bore the principal part in the debate, "is the dependence or independence of America." The address was adopted without a division.

In letters which arrived the next day from America, calumny, with its hundred tongues, exaggerated the turbulence of the people, and invented wild tales of violence; so that the king believed there was, in Boston, a regular committee for tarring and feathering; and that they were next, to use his own words, to "pitch and feather" Hutchinson himself. The press roused the national pride, till the zeal of the English people for maintaining English supremacy became equal to the passions of the ministry. Even the merchants and manufacturers were made to believe that their command of the American market depended on the enforcement of British authority.

It was, therefore, to a parliament and people as unanimous as when in Grenville's day they sanctioned the stamp act, that Lord North, on the fourteenth of March, opened the first branch of his American plan by a measure for the instant punishment of Boston. Its port was to be closed against all commerce until it should have indemnified the East India company, and until the king should be satisfied that for the future it would obey the laws. All branches of the government, all political parties, alike those who denied and those who asserted the right to tax, members of parliament, peers, merchants, all ranks and degrees of people, were invited to proceed steadily in the one course of maintaining the authority of Great Britain. Yet it was noticed that Lord North spoke of the indispensable necessity for vigorous measures with an unusual air of languor. This appeal was successful. Of the Rockingham party, Cavendish approved the measure, which was but a corollary from their own declaratory act. "After having weighed the noble lord's proposition well," said even Barré, "I cannot help giving it my hearty and determinate affirmative. I like it, adopt and embrace it for its moderation." "There is no good plan," urged Fox, "except the repeal of the taxes forms a part of it." "The proposition does not fully answer my expectations," said John Calvert; "seize the opportunity, and take away their charter."

On the eighteenth, Lord North, by unanimous consent, presented to the house the Boston port bill. To its second reading, George Bynge was the only one who cried no. "This bill," said Rose Fuller, in the debate, on the twenty-third, "shuts up one of the ports of the greatest commerce and consequence in the English dominions in America. The North Americans will look upon it as a foolish act of oppression. You cannot carry this bill into execution but by a military force." "If a military force is necessary," replied Lord North, "I shall not hesitate a moment to enforce a due obedience to the laws of this country." Fox would have softened the bill by opening the port on the payment of indemnity to the East India company; and he took care that his motion should appear on the journal. "Obedience," replied Lord North, "not indemnification, will be the test of the Bostonians." "The offence of the Americans is flagitious," said Van. "The town of Boston ought to be knocked about their ears and destroyed. You will never meet with proper obedience to the laws of this country until you have destroyed that nest of locusts." The clause to which Fox had objected was adopted without any division, and with but one or two negatives.

The current, within doors and without, set strongly against America. It was only for the acquittal of their own honor and the discharge of their own consciences that, two days later, on the third reading, Dowdeswell and Edmund Burke, unsupported by their former friends, spoke very strongly against a bill which punished the innocent with the guilty, condemned both without an opportunity of defence, deprived the laborer and the sailor of bread, injured English creditors by destroying the trade out of which the debts due them were to be discharged, and ultimately oppressed the English manufacturer. "You will draw a foreign force upon you," said Burke; "I will not say where that will end, but think, I conjure you, of the consequences." "The resolves at Boston," said Gray Cooper, "are a direct issue against the declaratory act;" and half the Rockingham party went with him. Rose Fuller opposed the bill, unless the tax on tea were repealed. Pownall was convinced that the time was not proper for a repeal of the duty on tea. "This is the crisis," said Lord North, who had by degrees assumed a style of authority and decision. "The contest ought to be determined. To repeal the tea duty or any measure would stamp us with timidity." "The present bill," observed Johnstone, late governor of West Florida, "must produce a confederacy, and will end in a general revolt." But it passed without a division, and very unfairly went to the lords as the unanimous voice of the commons. The king sneered at "the feebleness and futility of the opposition."

In the midst of the general anger, a book was circulating in England, on the interest of Great Britain in regard to the colonies, and the only means of living in peace and harmony with them, which judged the past and estimated the future with calmness and sagacity. Its author, Josiah Tucker, dean of Gloucester, a most loyal churchman, an apostle of free trade, saw clearly that the reduction of Canada had put an end to the sovereignty of the mother country; that it is in the very nature of all colonies, and of the Americans more than others, to aspire after independence. He would not suffer things to go on as they had lately done, for that would only make the colonies more headstrong; nor attempt to persuade them to send over deputies or representatives to sit in parliament, for that scheme could only end in furnishing a justification to the mother country for making war against them; nor have recourse to arms, for the event was uncertain, and England, if successful, could still never treat America as an enslaved people, or govern them against their own inclinations. There remained but one wise solution; and it was to declare the American colonies to be a free and independent people.

"If we separate from the colonies," it was objected, "we shall lose their trade." "Why so?" answered Tucker. "The colonies will trade even with their bitterest enemies in the hottest of a war, provided they shall find it their interest so to do. The question before us will turn on this single point: Can the colonists, in a general way, trade with any other European state to greater advantage than they can with Great Britain? If they cannot, we shall retain their custom;" and he demonstrated that England was for America the best market and the best storehouse; that the prodigious increase of British trade was due, not to prohibition, but to the suppression of monopolies and exclusive companies for foreign trade; to the repeal of taxes on raw materials; to the improvements, inventions, and discoveries for the abridgment of labor; to roads, canals, and better postal arrangements. The measure would not decrease shipping and navigation, or diminish the breed of sailors.

But, "if we give up the colonies," it was pretended, "the French will take immediate possession of them." "The Americans," resumed Tucker, "cannot brook our government; will they glory in being numbered among the slaves of the grand monarch?" "Will you leave the church of England in America to suffer persecution?" asked the churchmen. "Declare North America independent," replied Tucker, "and all their fears of ecclesiastical authority will vanish away; a bishop will be no longer looked upon as a monster, but as a man; and an episcopate may then take place." No minister, he confessed, would dare, as things were then circumstanced, to do so much good to his country; neither would their opponents wish to see it done; and "yet," he added, "measures evidently right will prevail at last."

A love of liberty revealed the same truth to John Cartwright. The young enthusiast was persuaded that humanity, as well as the individual man, obtains knowledge, wisdom, and virtue progressively, so that its latter days will be more wise, peaceable, and pious than the earlier periods of its existence. He was destined to pass his life in efforts to purify the British constitution, which, as he believed, had within itself the seeds of immortality. With the fervid language of sincerity, he advocated the freedom of his American kindred, and proclaimed American independence to be England's interest and glory.

Thus spoke the forerunners of free trade and reform. But the infatuated people turned from them to indulge unsparingly in ridicule and illiberal jests on the Bostonians, whom the hand of power was extended to chastise and subdue. At the meeting of the commons on the twenty-eighth, Lord North asked leave to bring in a bill for regulating the government of the province of Massachusetts Bay. On this occasion Lord George Germain showed anxiety to take a lead. "I wish," said he, "to see the council of that country on the same footing as that of other colonies. Put an end to their town-meetings. I would not have men of a mercantile cast every day collecting themselves together and debating about political matters. I would have them follow their occupations as merchants, and not consider themselves as ministers of that country. I would wish that all corporate powers might be given to certain people in every town, in the same manner that corporations are formed here. Their juries require regulation. I would wish to bring the constitution of America as similar to our own as possible; to see the council of that country similar to a house of lords in this; to see chancery suits determined by a court of chancery. At present their assembly is a downright clog; their council thwart and oppose the security and welfare of that government. You have no government, no governor; the whole are the proceedings of a tumultuous and riotous rabble, who ought, if they had the least prudence, to follow their mercantile employment, and not trouble themselves with politics and government, which they do not understand. Some gentlemen say: 'Oh, don't break their charter; don't take away rights granted them by the predecessors of the crown.' Whoever wishes to preserve such charters, I wish him no worse than to govern such subjects. By a manly perseverance, things may be restored from anarchy and confusion to peace, quietude, and obedience."

"I thank the noble lord," said Lord North, "for every one of the propositions he has held out; they are worthy of a great mind; I see their propriety, and wish to adopt them;" and the house directed North, Thurlow, and Wedderburn to prepare and bring in a bill accordingly.

On the twenty-ninth of March the Boston port bill underwent in the house of lords a fuller and fairer discussion. Rockingham, supported by the duke of Richmond, resisted it with firmness. "Nothing can justify the ministers hereafter," said Temple, "except the town of Boston proving in an actual state of rebellion." The good Lord Dartmouth called what passed in Boston commotion, not open rebellion. Lord Mansfield, a man "in the cool decline of life," acquainted only with the occupations of peace, a civil magistrate, covered with ermine that should have no stain of blood, with eyes broad open to the consequences, rose to take the guidance of the house out of the hands of the faltering minister. "What passed in Boston," said he, "is the last overt act of high treason, proceeding from our over-lenity and want of foresight. It is, however, the luckiest event that could befall this country; for all may now be recovered. Compensation to the East India company I regard as no object of the bill. The sword is drawn, and you must throw away the scabbard. Pass this act, and you will have passed the Rubicon. The Americans will then know that we shall temporize no longer; if it passes with tolerable unanimity, Boston will submit, and all will end in victory without carnage." In vain did Camden meet the question fully; in vain did Shelburne prove the tranquil and loyal condition in which he had left the colonies on giving up their administration. There was no division in the house of lords; and its journal, like that of the commons, declares that the Boston port bill passed unanimously.

The king in person made haste to give it his approval. To bring Boston on its knees and terrify the rest of America by enforcing the act, Gage, the military commander-in-chief for all North America, received the commission of civil governor of Massachusetts as swiftly as official forms would permit; and, in April, was sent over with four regiments, which he had reported would be sufficient to enforce submission. He was ordered to shut the port of Boston; and, having as a part of his instructions the opinion of Thurlow and Wedderburn, that acts of high treason had been committed there, he was directed to bring the ringleaders to condign punishment. Foremost among these, Samuel Adams was marked out for sacrifice as the chief of the revolution. "He is the most elegant writer, the most sagacious politician, and celebrated patriot, perhaps, of any who have figured in the last ten years," is the contemporary record of John Adams. "I cannot sufficiently respect his integrity and abilities," said Clymer, of Pennsylvania; "all good Americans should erect a statue to him in their hearts." Even where his conduct had been questioned, time proved that he had been right, and many in England "esteemed him the first politician in the world." He saw that "the rigorous measures of the British administration would the sooner bring to pass" the first wish of his heart, "the entire separation and independence of the colonies, which Providence would erect into a mighty empire." Indefatigable in seeking for Massachusetts the countenance of her sister colonies, he had no anxiety for himself, no doubt of the ultimate triumph of freedom; but, as he thought of the calamities that hung over Boston, he raised the prayer "that God would prepare that people for the event by inspiring them with wisdom and fortitude."

"We have enlisted in the cause of our country," said its committee of correspondence, "and are resolved at all adventures to promote its welfare; should we succeed, our names will be held up by future generations with that unfeigned plaudit with which we recount the great deeds of our ancestors." Boston has now no option but to make good its entire independence, or to approach the throne as a penitent, and promise for the future passive "obedience" to British "laws" in all cases whatsoever. In the palace there were no misgivings. "With ten thousand regulars," said the creatures of the ministry, "we can march through the continent."

The act closing the port of Boston did not necessarily provoke a civil war. It was otherwise with the second. The opinion of Lord Mansfield had been obtained in favor of altering the charter of Massachusetts; and the king learned "with supreme satisfaction" that, on the fifteenth of April, a bill to regulate the government of the province of Massachusetts Bay had been read for the first time in the house of commons. Without any hearing or even notice to that province, parliament was to change its charter and its government. Its institution of town-meetings was the most perfect system of local self-government that the world had ever known; the king's measure abolished them, except for the choice of town officers, or on the special permission of the governor. The council had been annually chosen in a convention of the outgoing council and the house of representatives, and men had in this manner been selected more truly loyal than the councillors of any one of the royal colonies; the clause in the charter establishing this method of election was abrogated. The power of appointing and removing sheriffs was conferred on the executive; and the trial by jury was changed into a snare, by intrusting the returning of juries to dependent sheriffs. Lord North placed himself in conflict with institutions sanctioned by royal charters, rooted in custom, confirmed by possession through successive generations, endeared by the just and fondest faith, and infolded in the affections and life of the people.

Against the bill Conway spoke with firmness. The administration, he said, would take away juries from Boston; though Preston, in the midst of an exasperated town, had been acquitted. They sent the sword, but no olive branch. The bill at its different stages in the house of commons was combated by Dowdeswell, Pownall, Sir George Saville, Conway, Burke, Fox, Barré, and most elaborately by Dunning; yet it passed the commons by a vote of more than three to one. Though vehemently opposed in the house of lords, it was carried by a still greater majority, but not without an elaborate protest. The king did not dream that by that act, which, as he writes, gave him "infinite satisfaction," all power of command in Massachusetts had, from that day forth, gone out from him, and that there his word would never more be obeyed.

The immediate repeal of the tax on tea and its preamble remained the only possible avenue to conciliation. On the nineteenth of April this repeal was moved by Rose Fuller in concert with the opposition. The subject in its connections was the gravest that could engage attention, involving the prosperity of England, the tranquillity of the British empire, the principles of colonization, and the liberties of mankind. But Cornwall, speaking for the ministers, stated the question to be simply "whether the whole of British authority over America should be taken away." On this occasion Edmund Burke pronounced an oration such as had never been heard in the British parliament. His boundless stores of knowledge came obedient at his command; and his thoughts and arguments, the facts which he cited, and his glowing appeals, fell naturally into their places; so that his long and elaborate speech was one harmonious and unbroken emanation from his mind. He first demonstrated that the repeal of the tax would be productive of unmixed good; he then surveyed comprehensively the whole series of the parliamentary proceedings with regard to America, in their causes and their consequences. After exhausting the subject, he entreated parliament to "reason not at all," but to "oppose the ancient policy and practice of the empire, as a rampart against the speculations of innovators on both sides of the question."

"Again and again," such was his entreaty, "revert to your old principles; seek peace and ensue it; leave America, if she has taxable matter, to tax herself. Be content to bind America by laws of trade; you have always done it; let this be your reason for binding their trade. Do not burden them by taxes; you were not used to do so from the beginning. Let this be your reason for not taxing. These are the arguments of states and kingdoms. Leave the rest to the schools. The several provincial legislatures ought all to be subordinate to the parliament of Great Britain. She, as from the throne of heaven, superintends and guides and controls them all. To coerce, to restrain, and to aid, her powers must be boundless."

During the long debate, the young and fiery Lord Carmarthen had repeated what so many had said before him: "The Americans are our children, and how can they revolt against their parent? If they are not free in their present state, England is not free, because

Manchester and other considerable places are not represented." "So, then," retorted Burke, "because some towns in England are not represented, America is to have no representative at all. Is it because the natural resistance of things and the various mutations of time hinder our government, or any scheme of government, from being any more than a sort of approximation to the right, is it therefore that the colonies are to recede from it infinitely? When this child of ours wishes to assimilate to its parent, are we to give them our weakness for their strength, our opprobrium for their glory? and the slough of slavery which we are not able to work off, to serve them for their freedom?"

The words fell from him as burning oracles; while he spoke for the rights of America, he seemed to prepare the way for renovating the constitution of England. Yet it was not so. Though more than half a century had intervened, Burke would not be wiser than the whigs of the days of King William. It was enough for him if the aristocracy applauded. He did not believe in the dawn of a new light, in the coming on of a new order, though a new order of things was at the door, and a new light had broken. He would not turn to see, nor bend to learn, if the political system of Somers and Walpole and the Pelhams was to pass away; if it were so, he himself was determined not to know it, but "rather to be the last of that race of men." As Dante sums up the civilization of the middle age so that its departed spirit still lives in his immortal verse, Burke idealizes as he portrays the lineaments of that old whig aristocracy which in its day achieved mighty things for liberty and for England. He that will study under its best aspect the enlightened character of England in the first half of the eighteenth century, the wonderful intermixture of privilege and prerogative, of aristocratic power and popular liberty, of a free press and a secret house of commons, of an established church and a toleration of Protestant sects, of a fixed adherence to prescription and liberal tendencies in administration, must give his days and nights to the writings of Edmund Burke. But time never keeps company with the mourners; it flies from the memories of the expiring past, though clad in the brightest colors of imagination; it leaves those who stand still to their despair, and hurries onward to fresh fields of action and scenes forever new.

Resuming the debate, Fox said, earnestly: "If you persist in your right to tax the Americans, you will force them into open rebellion." On the other hand, Lord North asked that his measures might be sustained with firmness and resolution; and then, said he, "there is no doubt but peace and quietude will soon be restored." "We are now in great difficulties," said Dowdeswell, speaking for all who adhered to Lord Rockingham; "let us do justice before it is too late." But it was too late. Even Burke's motive had been "to refute the charges against that party with which he had all along acted." After his splendid eloquence, no more divided with him than forty-nine, just the number that had divided against the stamp act, while on the other side stood nearly four times as many. The repeal of the tea-tax was never to be obtained so long as the authority of parliament was publicly rejected or opposed.

On the day on which the house of commons was voting not to repeal the duty on tea, the people of New York sent back the tea-ship which had arrived but the day before; and eighteen chests of tea, found on board of another vessel, were hoisted on deck and emptied into "the slip."

A third penal measure, which had been questioned by Dartmouth and recommended by the king, transferred the place of trial of any magistrates, revenue officers, or soldiers, indicted for murder or other capital offence in Massachusetts Bay, to Nova Scotia or Great Britain. As Lord North brought forward this wholesale bill of indemnity to the governor and soldiers, if they should trample upon the people of Boston and be charged with murder, it was noticed that he trembled and faltered at every word, showing that he was the vassal of a stronger will than his own, and vainly struggled to wrestle down the feelings which his nature refused to disavow. "If the people of America," said Van, "oppose the measures of government that are now sent, I would do as was done of old in the time of the ancient Britons: I would burn and set fire to all their woods, and leave their country open. If we are likely to lose it, I think it better lost by our own soldiers than wrested from us by our rebellious children." "The bill is meant to enslave America," said Sawbridge, with only forty to listen to him. "I execrate the present measure," cried Barré; "you have had one meeting of the colonies in congress; you may soon have another. The Americans will not abandon their principles; for, if they submit, they are slaves."

The bill passed the commons by a vote of more than four to one. But evil comes intermixed with good: the ill is evanescent, the good endures. The British government inflamed the passions of the English people against America, and courted their sympathy; as a consequence, the secrecy of the debates in parliament came to an end; and this great change in the political relation of the legislature to public opinion was the irrevocable concession of a tory government, seeking strength from popular excitement.

A fourth measure legalized the quartering of troops within the town of Boston. The fifth professed to regulate the affairs of the province of Quebec. The nation, which would not so much as legally recognize the existence of a Catholic in Ireland, from political considerations sanctioned on the St. Lawrence "the free exercise of the religion of the church of Rome, and confirmed to its clergy their accustomed dues and rights," with the tithes as fixed in 1672 by the edict of Louis XIV. But the act did not stop there. In disregard of the charters and rights of Massachusetts, Connecticut, New York, and Virginia, it extended the boundaries of the new government of Quebec to the Ohio and the Mississippi, and over the region which included, besides Canada, the area of the present states of Ohio, Michigan, Indiana, Illinois, and Wisconsin; and, moreover, it decreed for this great part of a continent an unmixed arbitrary rule. The establishment of colonies on principles of liberty is "the peculiar and appropriated glory of England," rendering her venerable throughout all time in the history of the world. The office of peopling a continent with free and happy commonwealths was renounced. The Quebec bill, which quickly passed the house of lords without an adverse petition or a protest, and was borne through the commons by the zeal of the ministry and the influence of the king, left the people who were to colonize the most fertile territory in the world without the writ of habeas corpus to protect the rights of persons, and without a share of power in any one branch of the government. "The Quebec constitution," said Thurlow, in the house of commons, "is the only proper constitution for colonies; it ought to have been given to them all, when first planted; and it is what all now ought to be reduced to."

In this manner Great Britain, allured by a phantom of absolute authority over colonies, made war on human freedom. The liberties of Poland had been sequestered, and its territory began to be parcelled out among the usurpers. The aristocratic privileges of Sweden had been swept away by treachery and usurpation. The free towns of Germany, which had preserved in that empire the example of republics, were "like so many dying sparks that go out one after another." Venice and Genoa had stifled the spirit of independence in their prodigal luxury. Holland was ruinously divided against itself. In Great Britain, the house of commons had become so venal that it might be asked whether a body so chosen and so influenced was fit to legislate even within the realm. If it shall succeed in establishing by force of arms its "boundless" authority over America, where shall humanity find an asylum? But this decay of the old forms of liberty was the forerunner of a new creation. The knell of the ages of servitude and inequality was rung; those of equality and brotherhood were to come in.

As the fleets and armies of England went forth to consolidate arbitrary power, the sound of war everywhere else on the earth died away. Kings sat still in awe, and nations turned to watch the issue.

4.

CHARLES KENDALL ADAMS

Charles Kendall Adams (1835-1902) was successively professor of history at the University of Michigan, president of Cornell University, and president of the University of Wisconsin. In 1898, when the United States had grown familiar with internal conflicts, both sectional and social, Adams took a new look at the American patriots who had carried on the revolt against Great Britain. Writing in 1898, he found the American cause less united and less worthy than had Bancroft.

This was one of the first of a long series of attacks on the Whig interpretation by a growing tribe of professional historians. Not all of the author's contentions have been borne out by subsequent investigations. For example, the most recent study of Lord George Germain refutes the charge of his neglect to send a crucial despatch to Burgoyne. It is also questionable that John Adams favored short enlistments in the Continental Army. But the direction of historical interpretation for several decades was that to which C. K. Adams here gave early expression. (Reprinted from The Atlantic Monthly, *Volume 82, August 1898, pp. 174-75, 177-89.)*

Some Neglected Aspects of the Revolutionary War

The people of every nation have their own way of writing history. With all the thoroughness and care of the German scholars, they have never been quite able to emancipate themselves so completely from certain fundamental proclivities as to present with impartiality all sides of the historical subject that happens to be under investigation. In France, Thiers glorifies the imperialism of Napoleon, and Lanfrey goes as far in the other direction. The Toryism of Hume and the Whiggism of Macaulay show that each took a retainer on his side. For such reasons, of the thousands of histories with which the world has been flooded, scarcely more than half a dozen can fairly be said to be alive after the lapse of a hundred years. When one has named the works of Herodotus, of Xenophon, of Thucydides, of Julius Cæsar, of Tacitus, and of Gibbon, what other historical books are there, more than a hundred years old, that can be said at the present day to have any real vitality?

It is to be feared that the United States has fared no better than other nations. The fierce democracy of Bancroft blinded him to the other side, and the federalism of Hildreth[1] gives to his work a kindred quality of partiality and incompleteness. However unconsciously, both were great advocates rather than great judges. Other historians have had the same defects, and the popular imagination has been obliged to feed itself upon representations more or less incomplete. Forty years or more ago, one of the foremost of American scholars remarked, before a large audience of university professors and students, that history must be rewritten from the American point of view. Although there may have been some reason for such a declaration, there seems to have been no need to give it special emphasis; for, whatever have been the defects of American historians, lack of patriotism has certainly not been one of them. It may well be doubted whether, in any one of the crucial periods of

[1] Richard Hildreth, author of *History of the United States* (6 vols. New York, 1856-60).

our history, the unsuccessful side has ever been adequately presented.

* * *

The school-books naturally present the most obvious events, and they are hardly to be condemned for failing to point out the hidden causes which are so often the potent factors of success and defeat. Thus, it has happened that certain very important phases of the war for independence have received scant consideration by those who have had much to do with framing public opinion. Moreover, there is nothing more sure than that the impressions which a child receives of the right and wrong of a dispute are difficult to eradicate.

One of the erroneous impressions lodged in the popular imagination is the supposed unanimity, or approach to unanimity, with which the Revolution was undertaken; and there is also a popular impression, equally erroneous, that the logical and the constitutional objections to the Revolutionary policy were weak and insignificant. The fact is that the Revolutionary War was a civil war in a far more strict and comprehensive sense than was the war between the states which broke out in 1861. But there has never been lodged in the popular imagination any adequate impression of the tremendous significance of those who always insisted upon calling themselves "Loyalists," but who were early stigmatized by their opponents with the opprobrious epithet of "Tories." Did we not all receive a nearly indelible impression from our juvenile reading that the Tories of the Revolution were men of such thoroughgoing badness that simple hanging was too good for them? It is now fair, however, to presume that we are far enough away from that exciting period to admit, without danger of bodily harm, that there were really two sides to the question as to whether fighting for independence was the more promising of the two policies open to the colonists. Until the appearance of Professor Tyler's Literary History of the Revolution,[2] who among the historians had fairly presented both sides of the case?

As usual in times of great excitement, the public was divided by more or less indefinite lines into several parties. These may be conveniently classified into four groups, — two on either side. Of

[2] Moses Coit Tyler, *A Literary History of the American Revolution* (New York, 1897).

those who were governors or other officials of the Crown, and consequently were ready to stand by the king through thick and thin, nothing need be said. But a second class of opponents to the Revolutionary movement was far more important, and is entitled to more careful consideration. Many, while fully admitting that the policy of the British government was in many respects bad, denied that forceful revolt was the proper way to remedy the evils. They believed, and until the outbreak of the war they boldly asserted, that a loyal and persistent support of the party led by Pitt, Burke, and Fox would finally result in the downfall of the "King's Friends" and the restoration of the Whigs, with all attendant advantages. They declared with confidence that open revolt would inevitably close the lips of those who in England sympathized with the American cause, and would drive all the members of Parliament to the support of the government in putting down what would be regarded as a rebellion. They declared also that in case of failure to secure the adoption of this policy by Parliament nothing would be lost, inasmuch as existing evils were far more than counterbalanced by existing benefits. They pointed out, moreover, that there was no evidence of a general disposition in England to oppress the colonists, and that there could be no lurking danger in the policy they advocated. There were many, too, who took the ground that in any event success by armed resistance was so overwhelmingly improbable as to be practicably impossible, and that an unsuccessful effort would probably augment the evils complained of.

Then, on the other hand, the Revolutionists, also, may be divided into two classes. There were those who protested earnestly against what they regarded as the oppressions of the mother country, but who, up to 1775, believed that reasonable protests would be met with reasonable replies and concessions. The leaders of this class were Washington and Franklin. Then there were those who at the beginning of the dispute were out-and-out advocates of resistance, and a little later out-and-out advocates of independence.

It is not strange that the latter class finally got the upper hand and secured the adoption of its policy. In times of intense political excitement it is the thoroughgoing who are apt to have their way. It was the Rhetts and the Yanceys who drew Lee and Stephens and the rest of the reluctant South after them into the whirlpool of 1861; and if they had succeeded, they would have been placed in that category of nationfounders in which Otis and Samuel Adams and Patrick Henry now occupy so lofty a position. After all, as has often been said, the most important difference between a revolution and a rebellion is the fact that the one justifies itself by success, while the other condemns itself by failure.

The importance of the Tory element in the Revolutionary War may be judged either by its numbers or by its respectability. Of the exact relative strength of the Tories and the Revolutionists it is not now easy to form a very confident opinion. Indeed, at the time of the war, in the absence of all machinery for taking a census of Loyalists and Revolutionists, the most careful estimate was not likely to be trustworthy. Two facts, however, are certain. One is that the Tories always claimed that if a census could have been taken, or if the question could have been fairly submitted to an unintimidated vote, it would have shown that a very considerable majority of the people throughout the country and throughout the entire war were opposed to the policy of resistance. The other fact is that those members of the Revolutionary party who had the best opportunity for observing and judging — men, for example, like John Adams, of Massachusetts, and Judge McKean, of Pennsylvania — believed that at least one third of the people were at all times opposed to the war. Moreover, it is obviously probable that many were Loyalists in secret. Indeed, it is well known that in all parts of the country and in all periods of the war many were in the habit of slinking away from the tar and feathers of the Revolutionists, and betaking themselves either stealthily out of the country, or to rocks and caves and other impenetrable hiding-places. Thus, the number of real opponents to the war may easily have been even greater than was apparent.

But aside from the opinions of contemporary judges, if we look into such evidences as are now available, we are forced to the same conclusion. No one can study the energetic and comprehensive measures of the various legislatures without seeing that the Tory element was formidable in numbers as well as in character. The records in Massachusetts show that the Tories were a constant source of anxiety and dread. In Connecticut the strength of the opposing element was still greater. In New York the Dutch and their retainers and supporters were, as a rule, so notoriously opposed to the war that the Tories in the aggregate certainly formed a very considerable majority of the population. Here is a typical example. Judge Jones, in describing the election of members to Congress in April, 1775, says: "The Loyalists, numbering three fourths of the legal voters, marched in a body to the polls, but their adversaries, having collected boys, unemployed sailors, and negroes, threatened all who opposed them. The result of this process was that a majority of the ballots cast were found to be in favor of the Revolutionary members." But even the methods of this patriotic mob as portrayed by Jones were not very successful; for in May of 1775 the New York Assembly passed resolutions approving of the course of the British ministry, — resolutions which gave great satisfaction in England, and went far to convince the government that the colonial opposition had been greatly exaggerated; that it was indeed insignificant, and could easily be overcome. In New York city, if Washington, soon after his arrival from Boston, had not sent a shivering chill through the enthusiastic opposition of the Tories by promptly hanging the foremost of their leaders, the Loyalist party might have been so successfully organized as to have kept the state solid in its support of the king. It was only this energetic action of Washington, supported as it was a little later by the similar energy of John Jay in judiciously banishing the most formidable of the Tory leaders, that finally brought the dominant forces of New York to the support of the war.

In Pennsylvania it was long doubtful whether the official support of the state could be given to the war movement; and that support was never very thorough or very enthusiastic. What Dr. Mitchell, in Hugh Wynne,[3] has represented as the condition in Philadelphia was the condition throughout the state. It is perhaps significant that when, not long after the evacuation of Philadelphia by Clinton, Arnold was placed in command of the city, he found the Tories in full social sway, and that he came so far under their influence as to fall in love with the most beautiful and accomplished of their daughters, — a proceeding preliminary to that alliance which, years afterward, caused his wife to be called "the saddest as well as the handsomest woman in England." His marriage with Margaret Shippen, however happy from a domestic point of view, yet gave an additional motive for Arnold's final plunge.

[3] *Hugh Wynne, Free Quaker* (New York, 1896), a historical novel by Silas Weir Mitchell.

Virginia seems to have had about the same proportion of Tories as Massachusetts. In North Carolina, the people, throughout the war, were nearly equally divided in their allegiance between the two Georges. South Carolina was Tory; and Georgia was so true to its royal namesake that the state not only refused to supply its quota of troops to the American George, but at the moment when the untoward event at Yorktown upset its calculations the legislature was on the point of denouncing the resistance as a failure, and giving its formal allegiance to the British side.

But it was not in numbers only that the Tories were formidable. They were even more formidable in influence, character, and respectability. It was natural, of course, that they should include not only the considerable class who held office under the king, but also a very large proportion of those whom we should now ban or bless by calling them conservatives. Thus it happened that in the Tory ranks were many clergymen, lawyers, physicians, as well as college graduates in general. Before the war, these men had been considered not only respectable, but eminent, in their several callings. Professor Tyler has admirably shown that even in the political literature of the day the Tories took an important part. While it must be admitted that in the production of the curious concoctions of rhyme and water which in those days passed for poetry the Revolutionary patriots took the lead, yet in elegant, forceful, logical prose, it is hard to see that the writings of such Loyalists as Boucher, Seabury, Leonard, and Galloway were inferior to those of Otis, Dickinson, Paine, and Adams; nevertheless, their writings have been quite forgotten.

But if we turn from literary merit, and consider simply the soundness or the unsoundness of their political and consitutional arguments, we shall find that they are still more worthy of consideration. Indeed, the drift of opinion of the most intelligent constitutional critics of today, in America as well as in England, is toward the view that in their constitutional arguments the Loyalist or Tory writers had a strong case. Naturally, the long succession of British constitutional lawyers, from Lord Mansfield down to Sir William Harcourt, have uniformly and almost if not quite unanimously held that, according to the immemorial custom of the realm, — that is, according to the British Constitution, — the enactments of the imperial Parliament, consisting of Crown, Lords, and

Commons, are constitutionally binding upon all British subjects. While they freely admit the authoritative force of the maxim, "No taxation without representation," they insist at all times that the maxim never has had, and has not now, the meaning that was attached to it by Otis, Dickinson, and the other colonial writers. They maintain that, in Parliament, the king, or the queen, represents all the members of the royal family; the House of Lords, all the members of the nobility; and the House of Commons, all the commonalty of the colonies as well as the mother country. According to the British theory, every member of the House of Commons represents no more truly the people who elect him than he does also all the other members of the commonalty, both in Great Britain and in the colonies. It was in accordance with this theory that the great cities of the manufacturing districts, which until recently had never sent a single member to the House of Commons, were held to be as truly represented as were London and York. This doctrine carried with it the same right to tax the colonies as to tax the citizens of Liverpool, Manchester, Birmingham, and Leeds; and the denial of that right by the colonial orators and essayists appears never to have made the least impression upon the constitutional lawyers of the mother country. Even Burke, who pleaded so eloquently and vehemently for conciliation with America, freely admitted, and never for a moment denied, that the government was acting within its constitutional rights. His contention was that, although Parliament possessed the constitutional right to impose taxation, it was nothing less than consummate madness to attempt to exercise that right, inasmuch as such action would inevitably, sooner or later, result in the loss of the colonies.

Now, this was exactly the ground taken by the American Tories, and exactly the opposite of the doctrine promulgated by the colonial writers on the Revolutionary side. There were two dominant notes in the contentions of the opponents of the British policy during the whole of the thirteen long years before the spring of 1776. The first was that the British Parliament had no constitutional right to tax the colonies; and the second, that it was the duty of the self respecting colonists to resist the exercise of every unconstitutional act. Accompanying these assertions was the emphatic and oft-repeated declaration that nobody sought or was in favor of independence. As late as the time when the first Continental Congress adjourned in October, 1775, the idea of independence met with no favor from Washington; and Franklin, who was then the American agent in London, assured the members of the British Parliament that he had "never heard of anybody, drunk or sober, who favored independence."

In view of all these facts, what wonder is it that the Tories, or what may be called the British party in America, contained within its ranks many of the most intelligent and the most highly educated people of the colonies? In 1778 the legislature of Massachusetts banished and confiscated the property of three hundred and ten of the most prominent of the Tory leaders of that state. Who were they? In scanning the list of names, Professor Tyler significantly remarks that it reads "almost like the bead-roll of the oldest and noblest families concerned in the founding and upbuilding of New England civilization." Dr. George E. Ellis, some years ago, pointed out the fact that in that list of three hundred and ten persons more than sixty were Harvard graduates. Nor was this exceptional. In the Middle States and in the South the Loyalist party contained a large representation of the graduates of Yale, Princeton, William and Mary, and Pennsylvania. Some of these were put to death, some were banished, and some were driven into hiding-places, whence, at the close of the war, they emerged only to be the targets of contempt and of all forms of abuse. A careful investigation of this phase of the contest will unquestionably lead every student to the conclusion that the ranks of the Tories contained a very considerable portion of the most thoughtful, the most intelligent, and the most refined of the colonial people.

That every effort should be made to destroy the power and the influence of these people while the war was going on was as natural as the attempt to make the cause successful. But, unfortunately, the severity of public opinion was not relaxed at the close of the war. Mr. Goldwin Smith has pointed out that there are special and exceptional reasons why the end of a civil war should always be followed by amnesty. But there was no amnesty at the close of the Revolutionary War. A single instance will serve as an example of the spirit that was shown. At the final evacuation of Charleston, after the treaty of peace had been signed, the departing British fleet took all the Tories it could carry. Those who, unhappily, were compelled to remain behind were subjected to the utmost indignities. "They were imprisoned, whipped, tarred and feathered, dragged through horse-ponds, and finally twenty-four of their number were hung upon a gallows in sight of the last of the retiring British." So strenuous was the public opinion of the patriots everywhere that even the protests of officers and other men of influence were in vain. General Greene declared that it was "an excess of intolerance to persecute men for opinions which twenty years before had been the universal belief of every class of society;" and John Jay denounced the "injudicious punishment and unmanly revenge," following the Revolution, as "without a parallel except in the annals of religious rage in the time of bigotry and blindness."

The effect of the spirit so generally shown in all parts of the country was injurious in many ways. Mrs. Anne Grant, the vivacious and intelligent Scotch lady who lived for many years in America, and then wrote her interesting and valuable book,[4] compares the loss of the colonies in expatriating the Loyalists after the Revolutionary War to the loss of the French in driving out the Huguenots after the Revocation; and Mr. Goldwin Smith, speaking of the fact that the expatriated Tories generally betook themselves, with all their rankling sense of injustice, to Nova Scotia, New Brunswick, and the Canadas, remarks that if a power hostile to the republic should ever be formed under European influence in the north of the continent, the Americans would owe such an event to their ancestors who refused amnesty to the vanquished in civil war.

There is another phase of the war to which attention has not perhaps been sufficiently called, namely, what might be termed fortuitous good fortune, — in Puritan phraseology, "special providence." It is military commonplace to remark that the issue of a battle often turns upon a very trifling circumstance. Napoleon used to say that in war a grain of sand would sometimes turn the scale; and yet that great commander was a firm believer in the doctrine that providence fights on the side of the heaviest battalions. But in the Revolutionary War providence often seemed to prefer the other side. Several times nothing less than the Puritan's "providential interposition" prevented a defeat, which might speedily have ended the contest. For instance, during the siege of

[4] *Memoirs of an American Lady* (2 vols. London, 1808).

Boston, although Tories and spies were everywhere, it was never revealed to the British that for several months the colonists had not ammunition enough for a single battle. If an assault upon the Americans had been made, it is difficult to see how the British could have failed of overwhelming success. So, too, after the battle of Long Island, when the capture of the entire American force seemed inevitable, the army was saved partly, no doubt, by the consummate skill of Washington in bringing the boats together, but partly, also, by a dense fog which enabled twelve thousand men, with all their guns and supplies, to cross the river without attracting the attention of the British pickets or the British fleet. When, a little later, in spite of Washington's vigorous exhortations and the flat side of his heavy sword, American recruits gave way on the first fire of the British at Kipp's Bay, the whole of his force in New York seemed to face inevitable annihilation. The British fleet guarded both shores of Manhattan Island, and the British army was above the Americans, opposite to what is now the East Thirty-Fourth Street Ferry. All that was needed to smother the American force, and apparently the American cause, was to march without delay across the island, and to hold the Americans with a large army in front and a naval force in the rear, as afterward Washington held Cornwallis at Yorktown. Howe's army was more than twice as large as Washington's; but the doom which the American commander with the flat and the edge of his sword could not prevent, the wit of Mrs. Murray, the resourceful mother of Lindley Murray, readily averted. Occupying the Murray country-seat, or mansion, as it was then called, on Murray Hill, she was directly in the line of the British march. The detention of the army for several hours by her tempting tea and other refreshments set before the officers enabled General Putnam, by a rapid movement up the west side of the island, to take the American force out of the trap before it was inexorably closed.

A still more striking instance of kindred nature was the reason why General Howe made his fatal move toward Philadelphia in 1777, instead of sending half of his troops northward to act with Burgoyne. The British plan of campaign, which resulted in the capture of the northern army, was so well designed and so comprehensive in its nature as to cause the most serious apprehensions. The plan to attack the Hudson from three directions — from Montreal, from Oswego, and from New York — certainly gave every promise of success. It failed simply for the reason that there was not proper cooperation of the three forces. In the absence of Howe's cooperation with Burgoyne, the people of New England and New York so generously destroyed the supplies upon which the enemy depended, and turned out in such force, as to compel the invaders either to starve or to surrender. Moreover, St. Leger, even after the defeat of Herkimer at Oriskany, was scared away from the siege of Fort Stanwix by the false report of American successes. These several failures could hardly have occurred but for one very curious incident.

The war office in London, as is now well known, having designed the campaign, issued general orders for the three expeditions; but, in giving preliminary directions to Sir William Howe, the department ordered him to await detailed instructions. These instructions were duly made out, directing him to divide his force, and to leave in New York only men enough to defend the city against any attacks that might be made by Washington, while with about half of his army he was to march north for the purpose of uniting and cooperating with Burgoyne. The plan threatened to cut off New England from the rest of the colonies, and also to rescue the state of New York. It is not easy to see how it could have failed if carried out as devised. But the final instructions to Howe did not arrive. His consequent inactivity made it possible for Schuyler at Albany, when he found that Burgoyne was likely to be taken care of, or at least was advancing so slowly through the woods to Whitehall as to cause no special anxiety, to send Arnold up the Mohawk to relieve Fort Stanwix and drive back the invading force under St. Leger. Arnold's success, it will be remembered, was so rapid and so complete as to enable him to return in time to play the leading part in the final entrapment of Burgoyne. Thus, so far as we can see, it was the delay of the anticipated orders of Howe that left Burgoyne to complet isolation and at the mercy of people who flocked to the standard of Gates.

But why did not these orders arrive? The reason was not discovered until afterward, when it was quite too late. It was found that the papers had been duly made out for the signature of the minister of war, Lord George Germain; but the punctilious fastidiousness of that officer was dissatisfied with the copy that had been prepared, and he ordered that a new and "fair" copy should be written out before he would sign it. When this copy was completed it was placed in the proper pigeon-hole to await the signature of the minister. Meantime, Lord George, having gone to his country-seat, was absent so long that on his return the order was not recalled to mind. After Howe, acting in accordance with the traitorous advice of General Charles Lee, had moved toward Philadelphia, and Burgoyne had surrendered, the order was rescued from its innocent pigeon-hole to mock the fastidiousness of the minister. Had the order been sent, who will undertake to say what its influence would have been on the fate of the Revolution?

One other example only will be offered. There is abundant reason to believe that the British government, as well as the British officers, regarded the war as practically at an end, when, in the early winter of 1776, New Jersey had been cleared and Washington had been driven south of the Delaware. Howe had received his knighthood for the capture of New York, and Cornwallis, thinking his services no longer needed, had sent his portmanteau on board a ship, with the purpose of embarking immediately for home. That audacious recrossing of the Delaware on Christmas night, which caused Frederick the Great to put Washington into the rank of great commanders, broke up the New York festivities, and called for immediate punishment. When Cornwallis's army played the return move, the Americans were in unquestionable peril. With the broad Delaware and its floating ice in Washington's rear, and a British army twice the size of his own in front, it is not difficult to understand why Cornwallis thought he had at last, as he said, "bagged the old fox." If the British commander had attacked vigorously on the afternoon of his arrival, as Washington, Grant, Lee, or any other great general would have done, the chances seem to have been more than ten to one that Washington and his whole army would have been taken prisoners. But Cornwallis was so sure of his game that he made the most stupendous blunder of the war, and decided to refresh his men by a night's sleep. It was a blunder precisely like that which prevented General W. F. Smith from taking Petersburg in June of 1864; and it appears to have been simply this mistake that enabled Washington not only to draw his army out of extreme peril, but also to fall upon the enemy at Princeton early the next morning, and, by threatening the British stores throughout the state, to force Cornwallis back into New York, and so, at the end of the campaign, to take possession of the whole of New Jersey with the exception of two or three stations on the Hudson. When Cornwallis finally surrendered at Yorktown, well might he express his admiration of the wonderful skill which had suddenly hurled an army four hundred miles with such accuracy and deadly effect, and then generously add, "But, after all, your excellency's achievements in New Jersey were such that nothing could surpass them."

One fact which, in the popular representations of the Revolutionary War, seems often either to have been overlooked or not to have been sufficiently emphasized, is the remarkable degeneration of Congress after the war had really begun. The first Continental Congress had brought together many of the very ablest men in the country. The colonies fully realized that questions of the utmost importance were to be considered, and they selected the best men as their representatives. With the possible exception of the Constitutional Convention, no other such body of men has ever yet come together in the history of the country. Its qualities went far to justify the remark of the elder Pitt to Franklin that it was "the most honorable assembly since the times of Greece and Rome."

But its successor was not of the same character. Moreover, for reasons which are not difficult to understand, a marked deterioration took place as time went on. As soon as the Declaration of Independence had been put forth, the people of the individual states began to think of organizing their own governments; and they naturally called into the service of constitution-making the ablest men they could command. To adopt thirteen new constitutions and to set thirteen new governments in motion made large drafts upon the available intelligence of the country.

Added to this depleting influence was the still further necessity of a strong representation in Europe. One has only to recall the names of those who were governors of states, and of those who were engaged in France, in Holland, and in Spain, between 1776 and 1783, to understand that if these men had been in Congress they would have furnished a swaying and a staying power of incalculable value. Then, too, the army had drawn into its ranks large numbers of prominent men who otherwise would have been in Congress. Nor can we forget what may as well be called the disaffected element. Samuel Adams, as soon as he had succeeded in fairly launching the Revolution, was so energetic in the exercise of his doctrine of state sovereignty that he seems to have dreaded the power of the confederated states scarcely less than he dreaded that of George III; and consequently he was an almost unceasing obstructionist to the cause of military efficiency. The fiery impatience of John Adams was as much in favor of the absurd and impossible policy of a "short and violent war" in the darkest period of the Revolution as was the impatience of Horace Greeley in 1862. Indeed, with the exception of Gouverneur Morris and John Jay, none of the members of Congress seem to have realized that the only practicable way of conducting the war to a successful close was the patient policy that was persistently followed by the commander-in-chief.

Now, a simple enumeration of these various facts is enough to show why it was that the second Continental Congress was so inferior to its great predecessor. When we look into its methods of dealing with the war, we ought not to be surprised to find that it was very far from being that unselfish body of intelligent patriots into which it seems to have been converted by the transforming and consecrating influence of time. On the contrary, it is not too much to say that one of the greatest difficulties that Washington had to contend with was the stupid, meddling, and obstructing inefficiency of those who sat at Philadelphia and at Yorktown for the supreme control of Continental affairs. At some of the meetings of that Congress not more than a dozen members were present, and these were often men of small ability and dogged pertinacity. It was almost harder for Washington to persuade — that is, to conquer — Congress than it was to conquer the British. One who looks through the long and pathetic series of letters of the great commander, and studies them with the single purpose of understanding the relations of Congress to the struggle that was going on, is likely to be amazed not only at the wisdom and tact of Washington, but at the almost infinite stupidities and difficulties with which he had to contend. The embarrassments that arose from these relations were partly political, but they were also largely military. New England, though it had heartily supported Washington at the beginning, found its courage oozing out and becoming lukewarm soon after the theatre of active operations was transferred to New York. It is not altogether strange that, while Washington was being driven from the centre of operations and steadily forced out of New Jersey, the New Englanders should point at what they could do at Bennington and Saratoga when they were energetically commanded; or that the New England sentiment, led by John Adams, had, in consequence, some sympathy with the Conway Cabal.

Neither Bancroft nor Hildreth nor any one of the older historians has adequately described the strength and the nature of the prevailing dissatisfaction. It is only in the light of letters and other documents that have become available within the past twenty years that we are able fully to understand the spirit of the time. Dr. Mitchell shows that spirit perfectly when he puts into the Diary of Jack Gainor these words: "Most wonderful it is, as I read what he wrote to inefficient, blundering men, to see how calmly he states his own pitiful case, how entirely he controls a nature violent and passionate beyond that of most men. He was scarcely in the saddle as commander before the body which set him there was filled with dissatisfaction." This expression of the novelist describes the situation better than do any of our historians, with the exception of John Fiske. It may be added that matters were brought to a favorable crisis only when Washington intimated that he might be driven to resignation, declaring, "It will be impossible for me to be of any further service, if such insuperable difficulties are thrown in my way."

Moreover, it was largely the short-sightedness as well as the energy of John Adams which led Congress to tolerate the policy of short enlistments. This policy Washington tried in every possible way to prevent, but his efforts were only partially successful. It was not till he failed in his appeals to Congress, and in his individual appeals to the governors of the various states, that he finally felt obliged to concentrate his views in the memorable Circular to States of October 18, 1780. What can be more instructive or suggestive than the following words? —

"We have frequently heard the behavior of the militia extolled upon one and another occasion by men who judge from the surface, by men who had particular views in misrepresenting, by visionary men whose credulity easily swelled every vague story in support of a favorite hypothesis. I solemnly declare I never was witness to a single instance that could countenance the opinion of militia or raw troops being fit for the real business of fighting. I have found them useful as light parties to skirmish in the woods, but incapable of making or sustaining a serious attack. This firmness is only acquired by habit of discipline and service. . . . We may expect everything from ours that militia is capable of, but we must not expect from them any services for which regulars alone are fit. The battle of Camden is a melancholy comment upon this doctrine. The militia fled at the first fire, and left the Continental troops, surrounded on every side and overpowered by numbers, to combat for safety instead of victory."

Not only was Congress inefficient in securing a proper organization, but it was equally inefficient in dealing with supplies. Later investigations have shown that the sufferings at Valley Forge did not arise from a general inadequacy of food and raiment, but from the fact that the commissariat department was so woefully remiss in the distribution of supplies where they were needed. It soon came to be known that at the very moment when thousands of Washington's troops were freezing and starving for want of blankets and food an abundant supply was accessible not many miles away. The mischief had been done when Congress, in opposition to Washington's advice, reorganized the commissariat department in 1777. At that time Congress decided to divide responsibility, and in place of Colonel Joseph Trumbull, who had been the successful head of the department, it put two men with coequal authority to do his work, — the one to make the purchases, and the other to distribute the supplies. Then, too, as if for the purpose of insuring chaos, the subordinate officers were made accountable to Congress rather than to the heads of the department. Colonel Trumbull, who was retained in one of the places, was soon so disgusted with the inevitable results that he resigned. Is it strange that at one time the army was two days without meat, and three days without bread?

The quartermaster's department was scarcely better. It was afterward ascertained that at the very time when, as Washington wrote, twenty-eight hundred and ninety-eight men were "unfit for duty because they were barefoot and otherwise naked," "hogsheads of shoes, stockings, and clothing were lying at different places on the roads and in the woods, perishing for want of teams, or of money to pay the teamsters."

But even worse than all this, those who provided the supplies were tainted with peculation and fraud. The historical student, as he gives up the idea that the legislation of the time was supremely wise, must also, however reluctantly, abandon the idea that the Revolutionary period was an age of spotless political virtue. Again and again Washington pleaded with Congress and with the chief officers of the individual states. In appealing to President Reed, of Pennsylvania, on the 12th of December, 1778, to bring those whom he calls the "murderers of our cause" "to condign punishment," he unbridled his passion and sent these energetic words: "I would to God that one of the most atrocious in each state was hung in gibbets upon a gallows five times as high as the one prepared by Haman." The situation seemed so desperate that, only six days later, he wrote to Benjamin Harrison, Speaker of the House of Delegates of Virginia, "As there can be no harm in a pious wish for the good of one's country, I shall offer it as mine that each state will not only choose, but compel their ablest men to attend Congress."

But Washington's prayer, for this once at least, was not answered. When, as time wore on, the French ministers arrived, they naturally had little difficulty in playing upon the credulity and simple-mindedness of the members. It is now well known that the policy of France in the alliance was twofold. She not only insisted that the colonies should not make peace until independence was recognized, but she was secretly determined that the colonies should not be so overwhelmingly successful as to endanger the interests of France and her allies by including the Canadas and the territories lying in the West and South. This latter phase of French policy, revealed as it has been by the publication of the correspondence between the French government and their ministers in America, has made it certain that Gérard, Marbois, and Luzerne employed all those arts of dissimulation, as well as of flattery, which have been called the *mensonge politique*. The letters of Vergennes to the envoys contain frequent references to *donatifs,* and those of de Circourt to *sécours temporaires en argent*. These expressions refer unmistakably to bribery, for Vergennes writes to Luzerne, "His Majesty further empowers you to continue the gifts which M. Gérard has given or promised, and of which he will surely have handed you a list." The list of persons here referred to, who were to be persuaded with money, has not been disclosed; but Durand tells us that Tom Paine, who was then the secretary of the Committee on Foreign Affairs, and of course knew all its secrets, was engaged by the

French minister, for a thousand dollars a year, "to inspire the people with sentiments favorable to France." No doubt the rascal earned his money, but who the other members were that were thus inspired we do not know. That such "inspiration," however, was used to a greater or less extent there can be no possible doubt. One of the biographers of John Jay relates that, some thirty years after the events here mentioned, Gouverneur Morris went over from Morrisania to visit his old friend Jay at Bedford. During their conversation Morris suddenly ejaculated through clouds of smoke, "Jay, what a set of damned scoundrels we had in that second Congress!" "Yes," said Jay, "that we had," and the venerable ex-Chief Justice knocked the ashes from his pipe.

But perhaps the most important of all the neglected phases of the Revolutionary struggle is the stupendous fact that Great Britain was prevented from prosecuting the war with vigor by complications in Europe. It would only partially express the truth to say that England fought the colonies with one hand tied behind her, or even to declare that it was only her left hand that was free. No adequate impression of the relations of the forces engaged can be obtained without keeping constantly in mind several all important facts that have too often been neglected.

It is necessary to remember that France had but recently been as bitterly humiliated by England as she was a century later by Germany. Those marvelous years of the domination of the elder Pitt had not only converted the Kingdom of England into the British Empire, but had accomplished this prodigious result mainly at the expense of France. It was from the French that India was taken by Clive and Pocock, as Canada was taken by Wolfe and Saunders. Not only was France stripped of her magnificent colonial possessions in Africa, as well as in Asia and America, but she saw her navy everywhere defeated and dispersed, and her commerce completely destroyed. These events had occurred less than twenty years before the outbreak of the American war; and the natural consequence was that the hostile feelings of the people of France toward England from 1763 to 1778 were quite as intense as the feelings of the same people toward Germany during the fifteen years after the treaty of 1871. Everybody now knows that if, during that period, Germany had in any way become seriously involved with a foreign power, the French would have seized the opportunity to wipe out the humiliation that had overwhelmed them at Sedan and Paris. Of kindred nature had been the relations of England and France a hundred years before.

But even this was not all. The attitude of England in regard to the right of search had made her practically the enemy of every one of the European powers. While for some years there was no outbreak, it was evident that nothing but the utmost circumspection could prevent a hostile alliance of the most formidable character. The fact that Catherine II was prevented from a declaration of war only by the earnest advice of Frederick the Great shows that there was not a little danger of a general European conflagration. Moreover, the English entered upon the American war with a full knowledge of all this rankling hatred upon the part of France, and of the certainty that if at any time the French should see an opportunity to interfere with success they would not fail to do so, and in all probability would draw several of the other European nations after them.

Nor must it be supposed that France had been so completely and permanently crippled as no longer to be formidable. Indeed, the nation had recovered from the material disasters of 1759 nearly as rapidly as, more than a century later, she recovered from the disasters of 1871. But, as their strength grew, the French seemed to remember all the more vividly that their navy had been ruined, root and branch, and that whenever a French merchantman had ventured out of port it had been pounced upon by some watchful British cruiser. The "armed neutrality" of the Baltic powers had not yet been directed against the supremacy of the sea power of England, and consequently not a ship of any nation, suspected of transporting goods out of a French port or destined to it, was exempt from search and confiscation; nor could it be forgotten that it was to counteract this exercise of what seemed like omnipotence as well as omniscience that the family compact was made which bound Spain to declare war against England within a year after war was declared by France. It has not always been remembered by American historians that it was chiefly the discovery of this secret alliance by Pitt, and the opposition of the headstrong young king to the measures by which the great minister proposed to thwart the alliance, that led to Pitt's downfall, and the substitution of Newcastle and Bute in his place.

Moreover, the situation was aggravated by certain other very irritating conditions. On the one hand, the needless failure of Byng to relieve Minorca, and the consequent fall of that important island into the hands of the French, was a source of such infinite chagrin to the English that it could not be wiped out by the mere execution of an admiral; while, on the other hand, the possession of Gibraltar by the British was so constant a humiliation to the Spanish that an offensive and defensive alliance between France and Spain was the inevitable consequence of the situation. These inflammatory elements were so menacing that Pitt, at one time, made the remarkable proposal to Spain to give up Gibraltar as the price of an alliance for the recovery of Minorca. The mere fact that such terms were offered is enough to show the gravity of the situation. At least, it may be said that if the answer of Spain had been different, either France would never have gone to the help of America, or in doing so she would have had Spain as an enemy rather than as an ally. But, whatever the course of France, the union of England and Spain might easily have turned the scale of the war; for, without the French alliance, it is impossible to see how the colonies could have escaped from being overwhelmed by England and Spain combined. Even if France were not prevented from the alliance, her fleet could not have stood against the united navies of England and Spain; the expedition of de Grasse would have been impossible, and the Yorktown campaign could not have occurred. Thus, it is easy to see that if Pitt's proposal had been accepted England might not only have regained Minorca, but might also have retained the American colonies. Such a result would hardly have been a dear purchase even at the tremendous price of Gibraltar.

The main significance of all these conditions for our purpose is the fact that the English knew of the discoveries of Pitt; that they were fully aware that Spain and probably other European nations would be allied with France whenever the French government should see fit to go to the assistance of the revolting colonies. As is well known, the consummation of this twofold project would have occurred much earlier than it did but for the natural reluctance of Louis XVI to assist organized opposition to royal authority. These conditions, moreover, explain why it was that while England had not less than two hundred thousand men under arms, on land and sea, not more than about twenty thousand of them could be spared for the war in America. They also explain why it was that England decided to resort to the unusual method of using a part of the vast wealth she had recently acquired by her commercial supremacy for the employment of mercenary troops from Germany.

From the letters and other papers that are now coming to us in authentic form and in rich abundance, we are learning more perfectly than ever before how it was that the Revolution was achieved. These revelations seem likely to teach us that from the beginning to the very end the Revolution was a far more desperate and a far more doubtful struggle than the historians have led us to believe. They teach us also that it was kept from the disaster that seemed again and again ready to overwhelm it, chiefly by that watchful wisdom of Washington which, to use Goethe's phrase, was as unhasting and as unresting as the stars.

5.

J. FRANKLIN JAMESON

A characteristic of historical writing in the first half of the twentieth century was a much greater attention than had previously been given to economic considerations. Charles Beard discovered economic motives in the drafting of the United States Constitution, James Truslow Adams in the founding of New England, and a host of writers in various aspects of the American Revolution. Accompanying this trend was a tendency to see in nearly every period a conflict between social classes, arising from economic differences.

On the two hundred and fiftieth anniversary of independence, J. Franklin Jameson, one of the outstanding professional historians of his day, delivered a series of four lectures at Princeton University on The American Revolution Considered as a Social Movement, *the title under which they were subsequently published. In this brief study Jameson reopened the question which Friedrich Gentz had discussed more than a century earlier and concluded that the American Revolution bore a good deal more resemblance to the French Revolution than Gentz or other historians had recognized. The American Revolution, Jameson suggested, had been in some measure at least, a movement of lower against upper classes and had brought sweeping social changes in the direction of a leveling of class distinctions and an increase of democracy. Though some of Jameson's conclusions were based on studies that have since proved unreliable, his remains the classic interpretation of the Revolution as a social movement. The first chapter (pages 1-39) outlines his thesis and contains some of his more arresting propositions. (Reprinted from J. Franklin Jameson,* The American Revolution Considered as a Social Movement, *by permission of Princeton University Press. Copyright 1926, by Princeton University Press.)*

The Revolution and the Status of Persons

In this year 1925 we enter upon a long series of celebrations commemorating the one hundred and fiftieth anniversaries of the successive events of the American Revolution. If any of those present are able, like myself, to remember well the long series of centennial commemorations of those same events, that marked the years from 1875 to 1883, and even to 1889, they will, I think, agree with me that those celebrations did more than anything else that has happened in our life-time to stimulate popular interest in American history in general, and specifically in the history of the American Revolution. The *Magazine of American History* was founded at once, in 1876. The Daughters of the American Revolution, a more numerous body than ever before were united in the commemoration of any portion of history, and the two societies of Sons, date from that period. A still wider, though indirect, indication of popular historic interest may be seen in the passion for what is called "colonial" furniture, a passion which distinctly flowed from these commemorations and especially from the Philadelphia Centennial of 1876, for it is certain that down to that year the sway of black walnut and funereal horsehair was steadily maintained. A less popular but more fruitful blossoming of interest in history may be seen in the striking rapidity with which, in the 'eighties immediately succeeding, professorships of history were established in the American colleges and universities, and in the sudden zeal with which numbers of able young students devoted themselves to the study of their country's history.

The consequences which flowed from the celebrations of fifty years ago are so far certain to repeat themselves in our time, that we may at least be sure of a speedy heightening of interest in the history of the American Revolution. The main desire that has underlain the preparation of the ensuing lectures has been the wish that whatever results, whether in learned academic research or in popular thinking, may spring from this new period of commemorations, may be marked by a wider view of the events than was taken fifty years ago. Surely it ought to be so, in view of the advances which history has made in America in fifty years, from a time when there were probably not a dozen professional students of history in the United States to a time when there are at least several hundreds.

The gain, the wider view, should show itself in three ways. In the first place, it ought to be possible for us to be much fairer to the British or Loyalist opponents of our fathers than were the men of fifty years ago. They had hardly emancipated themselves from the traditional view, generated in the heat of the old conflict, that the British statesmen of that time were monstrous tyrants, the British soldiers monstrous barbarians. There is, to be sure, an opinion abroad that the permanent maintenance of that view is an essential trait of American patriotism. It is conceded that in the study of every other war—of Athens against Sparta, or Rome against Carthage, or Parliamentarian against Royalist, or Prussia against France, or Union gainst Confederacy—it is the duty of rational beings to hear both sides, and not to suppose that the ultimate truth of history is to be gathered by listening solely to the immediate war-cries of one of the two contestants. An historical student who has no special affection for England, but on the other hand is not seeking any office for which he needs Irish-American votes, cannot help raising in some perplexity the question why the common-sense rules of fairness should be inapplicable to this war alone among all wars, why our histories of it should be sedulously guarded against improvement, or why writers who take a modern and detached view of it should be accused of the covert reception of British gold.

Another advance that we ought to make consists in a revision of the popular estimate of the men of Revolutionary times. Fifty years ago, and even a hundred years ago, there had become fixed in the public mind the notion that, because in the period of the Revolution there were many heroic characters and deeds, the whole American population of that time was heroic. It is pleasant to think well of a whole generation of those who have preceded us, and especially pleasant to glorify them if they were our ancestors. It may seem harmless, but when it is done in terms of comparison with later generations it is not altogether wholesome. It is not wholesome because it is not just. Nothing can be more certain than that, if we consider the whole nation and not merely the individual instances of heroic character and conduct, the patriotism of 1861, on both sides, was much more widely extended and more ardent than the much-lauded patriotism of 1776, and that of 1918 more pervasive, more enlightened, and more pure than either. How could we expect it to be otherwise, when we consider carefully the circumstances of the time? Let us distinguish between the heroes who fought and suffered and made every sacrifice to bring into existence a new nation, and the population at large, of whom so great a proportion were, as a matter of fact, however we may excuse them, provincial-minded, dubious in opinion, reluctant to make any sacrifices, half-hearted in the glorious cause. All honor to the heroes, and they were many.

> We sit here in the Promised Land,
> That flows with Freedom's honey and milk;
> But 'twas they won it, sword in hand,
> Making the nettle danger soft for us as silk.

But let us not forget that a large part of their heroism had to be expended in overcoming difficulties which need not have existed but for the slackness and indifference of their fellows. For instance, no episode of the history of the Revolution affords a finer example of patriotic sacrifice than the winter's encampment at Valley Forge; but why were the sufferings at Valley Forge encountered? Simply because the country at large, with whatever excuses, did not support the war, and the army which was waging it, with any approach to the ardor which was shown in 1861, on both sides, or in 1918. Clothes and shoes and blankets and tents were lacking. Who does not know what would happen if an American army of the present day were found to be destitute even of chocolate drops? It would not be three days before the metropolitan dailies would be voicing loudly a nation's wrath, and car-loads of chocolate drops would be rushed promptly to every camp. Let us be fair to the moderns, and not fabricate an imaginary golden age in the undeveloped America of 1776.

Thirdly, and closer to the immediate purpose of these lectures, it is to be wished that in the coming commemorations and in our future thinking we may consider the American Revolution in broader aspects than simply the political and the military. Fifty years ago, it was these that engrossed attention, and indeed most that has been written since then about the Revolution has been narrowly confined to these two aspects, the political and the military, including of late the naval. Every move in the political struggle for independence from Great Britain, every action of the Continental Congress, has been described over and over again. Every battle and every skirmish in that long and dragging war has had its historian, or has been the theme of meticulous articles or controversial pamphlets. Meanwhile, even in this age when social history is so much in fashion all over the world, few writers have concerned themselves with the social aspects of our American revolutionary history.

How different is it with the Frenchmen's study of the great French Revolution! Forty or fifty years ago they were in much the same state as we: every move of the politicians, every picturesque happening in Paris, every march or engagement of the revolutionary armies, was eagerly chronicled by intelligent but more or less conventional historians; but in more recent years the horizon of the French historians of their revolution has broadened, and more attention has been given to the prodigious effects of the French Revolution upon the constitution of French society than to the political events, more to the march of the revolutionary ideas than to the march of the revolutionary battalions, and quite as much to the progress of the revolution in the provinces as to the dramatic events that marked its development in Paris. The result has been that the French Revolution is now seen in its true proportions and effects, not simply as the downfall of monarchy or the securing of equal political rights for all individuals, but chiefly as a social movement, French and European, of vast dimensions and of immense significance.

Perhaps some may be moved to say at once: But this is precisely to ignore the most salient contrast between the American Revolution and the French. The men of our Revolution, they will say, were neither levellers nor theorists. Their aims were distinctly political, not social. They fought for their own concrete rights as

Englishmen, not for the abstract rights of man, nor for liberty, equality, and fraternity. The French rose in revolt against both a vicious political system and a vicious social system. With enthusiastic ardor they proceeded to sweep away abuses of all sorts, and to create, not simply a new government, but a new France and indeed, to their own imaginations, a new heaven and a new earth. That they cared more for the social than for the political results of the Revolution was evident when, after a few years, believing it impossible to retain both, they resigned political freedom and threw themselves into the arms of the young Corsican who gave promise of preserving for them their new social system. Not so, it will be said, the Anglo-Saxon. He had no wish to destroy or to recast his social system. He sought for political freedom, but he had no mind to allow revolution to extend itself beyond that limited sphere. As Burke said, he was "taught to look with horror on those children of their country who are prompted rashly to hack that aged parent to pieces and put him into the kettle of magicians, in hopes that by their poisonous weeds and wild incantations they may regenerate the paternal constitution."

It is indeed true that our Revolution was strikingly unlike that of France, and that most of those who originated it had no other than a political programme, and would have considered its work done when political independence of Great Britain had been secured. But who can say to the waves of revolution: Thus far shall we go and no farther? The various fibres of a nation's life are knit together in great complexity. It is impossible to sever some without also loosening others, and setting them free to combine anew in widely different forms. The Americans were much more conservative than the French. But their political and their social systems, though both were, as the great orator said, still in the gristle and not yet hardened into the bone of manhood, were too intimately connected to permit that the one should remain unchanged while the other was radically altered. The stream of revolution, once started, could not be confined within narrow banks, but spread abroad upon the land. Many economic desires, many social aspirations were set free by the political struggle, many aspects of colonial society profoundly altered by the forces thus let loose. The relations of social classes to each other, the institution of slavery, the system of land-holding, the course of business, the forms and spirit of the intellectual and religious life, all felt the transforming hand of revolution, all emerged from under it in shapes advanced many degrees nearer to those we know.

These are only assertions. They cannot be adequately proved in a few lectures. It will content the lecturer if he can partially illustrate their truth, and if some who hear him are convinced that here is a field of history deserving further and deeper study. Meantime we might profitably consider for a moment whether it is intrinsically probable that our revolution was unlike other popular revolutions, in having no social results flowing from the political upheaval. Is there such a thing as a natural history of revolutions? Nation differs from nation, and age from age, but there are some uniformities in human nature, some natural sequences recurrently presenting themselves in human history. Not all political revolutions, it is true, have had important social consequences. One notable variety of revolution is that whereby one reigning individual or one small group of individuals holding supreme power is supplanted by another individual or small group, without any serious alteration of the system. Such are those "palace revolutions" whereby Jehu the son of Nimshi succeeds Jehoram the son of Ahab, or the tsar Alexander supplants the tsar Paul, without more disturbance of the social system than when "Amurath to Amurath succeeds" in a wholly peaceable manner. But it is the other variety, popular revolutions, which we have in mind. This is the variety which figures most largely in modern history. A popular revolution usually consists in the transfer of political power from the hands of a smaller into those of a larger mass of the citizens, or from one great section of the population to another. As the result of such a revolution, we expect to see the new group exercising its new-found power in accordance with its own interests or desires, until, with or without fixed intention of so doing, it alters the social system into something according better with its own ideals. After the peaceful English revolution known as the passing of the Parliamentary Reform Act of 1832, we look to see the new Parliament, chosen by a wider suffrage and representing now the middle classes, passing a mass of legislation that brings the social state of England into better conformity with middle-class ideals. After the American Civil War, which shifted the seat of political power from the planting aristocracy of the South to the manufacturing and commercial classes of the North, we look to see legislation and the growth of custom whereby the American social system takes on forms congenial to the minds of the new possessors of power. But indeed we do not need to look farther into the past than the last nine years, to observe how the greatest of all revolutions, the one destined evidently to be the most momentous in its consequences, beginning with the overthrow of a tsar and the substitution of a republic, speedily escapes from the control of those who would keep it purely or mainly political, and transforms Russian society by 1925 to an extent which no one would in 1913 have dreamed to be possible.

If then it is rational to suppose that the American Revolution had some social consequences, what would they be likely to be? It would be natural to reply that it depends on the question, who caused the Revolution, and that therefore it becomes important to inquire what manner of men they were, and what they would be likely, consciously or unconsciously, to desire. In reality, the matter is not quite so simple as that. Allowance has to be made for one important fact in the natural history of revolutions, and that is that, as they progress, they tend to fall into the hands of men holding more and more advanced or extreme views, less and less restrained by traditional attachment to the old order of things. Therefore the social consequences of a revolution are not necessarily shaped by the conscious or unconscious desires of those who started it, but more likely by the desires of those who came into control of it at later stages of its development.

You know how it was with the English Revolution of the seventeenth century. At first it was the affair of moderate statesmen, like Pym and Hampden, or moderate generals like Essex or Manchester, earls, who would not push the king too hard, but before long it fell into the hands of men like Cromwell, whose spirit is shown by his bold declaration, "If I should meet the king in battle, I would as soon fire my pistol at him as at any man." Now when we examine the interesting mass of constitutional and social legislation enacted by the parliaments of the Commonwealth, we see in it the work of men of far more advanced views than those of Pym and Hampden, to wit, of radicals who had come into control of the movement in its latest stages.

Or again, take the French Revolution. Everyone knows how its history is marked by distinct successive periods, in each of which the control is exercised by a group more radical and extreme than its predecessors; and the same has been true of the great Russian revolution. Now, widely as our American Revolution differed from these, do not let us suppose that it escaped every trait of conformity to the natural history of such movements. Certain it is that, in some of our states at least, it fell ultimately into quite other hands than those that set it in motion.

Well, then, we may ask, who were in favor of the Revolution, and who were against it? The answer of course varies with the different stages of its development. In 1774 the partisans of American independence were very few, though there had long been those who thought, in an academic way, that it would soon take place. In most years after 1776 the partisans of American independence were the great majority. But what sort of man became a Tory as it gradually became necessary to take sides? What sort of man became a Whig? As a matter of course, almost all persons who enjoyed office under the Crown became Tories, and these were a large number. In an age when the king's turnspit was a member of Parliament, and under a king whose chief means of political action was the distribution of offices, office-holders were certain to be numerous, and their pay was, in proportion to the wealth of the country and the work they had to do, much greater than it is now. If the natural desire of all mankind to hold on to a lucrative office (a desire which is said sometimes to influence political action even in this age) did not make an office-holder a Tory, there was another motive arising from the fact that he had been appointed and had sworn to execute the laws, and might therefore feel in duty bound to obey the instructions of the ministers in England. As for the merchants, many, who had extensive interests that were imperilled by rebellion, adhered to the royal cause. But on the whole the great body of the merchants of the thirteen colonies were Whigs, for of the deep underlying causes, which for a generation had been moving the American mind in the direction of independence, none was so potent, according to all the best testimony, as the parliamentary restrictions on the trade of the colonies. Among farmers many of the richest took the royalist side. Probably most Episcopalians did so, except in the South. Everywhere the debtor class was, as was natural, and as has been true the whole world over, mainly on the side of revolution.

If we speak of professions, we should note that probably most of the clergy were Whigs, with the exception of nearly all the clergymen of the Church of England in the northern colonies. Most lawyers were Whigs, but most of the most eminent and of those enjoying the largest practice were Tories. John Adams says that, of the eight lawyers who had an important practice before the Superior Court of Massachusetts at the time of the Stamp Act, only Otis and he were Whigs ten years later. One of the others had died, and the remaining five were Tories. Among physicians the proportion of Tories was quite as large as among lawyers.

A word as to race and nationality. Colonists who had very recently arrived from England were likely to take the Tory side. Immigrants from Scotland, also, were usually Tories. A hundred and fifty years ago the Scots at home were among the warmest of Tories; Hume's *History of England* is typical of their feelings. Perhaps, too, their well-known clannishness gave them, in America, the position of aliens who held together, and would not assimilate with the rest of the population. Of the Irish, on the other hand, and those of the Scotch-Irish stock, Protestants from the north of Ireland, it is customary to hold that they were warmly and by vast majority on the side of revolution. It is not so certain. Industrious efforts have been made to show that they formed the backbone of the Revolutionary army—efforts partly based on a misinterpretation of a single passage in Joseph Galloway's testimony before a committee of the House of Commons. On the other hand, I have observed that, in the two large lists of Loyalist claimants that give the country of birth, 146 out of 1358 claimants, or eleven per cent, say that they were born in Ireland—a larger number than were born in England. Yet in Pennsylvania, where the proportion of Irish or Scotch-Irish population was greatest, it was unquestionably their influence that carried the state for independence, at the same time breaking the power in state affairs of the Philadelphia conservatives, and bestowing upon the state a radically democratic constitution. In all the colonies the Germans generally adhered to the party of independence, but not with great ardency.

As is usually the case, the revolutionary side was more frequently espoused by young men, the conservative cause by their elders. There were not a few conspicuous cases, such as that of Sir John Randolph, the king's attorney-general in Virginia, and his son

Edmund Randolph, in which the son adopted the former, the father the latter cause, and other cases, like that of Samuel and Josiah Quincy, in which an elder and a younger brother were thus divided. Among all the leaders of the Revolution, very few were forty-five years old in 1775; most were under forty. But think for a moment of the leaders of the French Revolution—Robespierre thirty-one years old when the Revolution began, Danton thirty, Camille Desmoulins twenty-seven, Collot-d'Herbois thirty-nine, Couthon thirty-three, Lebas twenty-four, Saint-Just twenty-one—and we shall see cause to be glad that our Revolution was carried through by men who, though still young, had at any rate reached their full maturity of thought and of character.

If we should investigate the Tory party in the several colonies in detail, we should be forced to the conviction that, in New England, it comprised in 1775 a very great share, probably more than half, of the most educated, wealthy, and hitherto respected classes. In March 1776, when Howe evacuated Boston, eleven hundred refugees sailed away with him. These eleven hundred, and the thousand or more who subsequently followed them, bore away perhaps a majority of the old aristocracy of Massachusetts. The act of banishment which the state legislature passed in 1778, to punish the Tories, includes among its three hundred-odd names some representatives of most of the families which had been distinguished in the earlier days of the colony. The loss of this important element, cultivated, experienced, and public-spirited, was a very serious one. It is true that many Tories returned after the war, but their fortunes were usually much broken, and they could never regain their influence. In New England, in short, it appears that the Revolution brought new strata everywhere to the surface.

In New York it seems probable that, in the height of the war at least, the bulk of the property-owners belonged to the Tory party, and it was strong also among the middle classes of the towns and among the country population. On the large manorial estates the tenant farmers sided with their landlords if they took sides at all. The city of New York and the county of Westchester were strongly Tory during at least the period of the British occupation, and Westchester very likely before. So were Staten Island and the three counties of Long Island.

In Pennsylvania it is probable that during the critical years of the war, at least, the majority of the population was on the side of the Crown, and that majority seems to have included many persons of eminence, and many Quakers. On the other hand, as is well known, the Virginian aristocracy in general, living somewhat remote from the influence of the royal officials, upon their secluded estates, were full of the spirit of local independence. Quite unlike their New England compeers, they took the Whig side, and that almost unanimously. It was the Virginian planters who formed the local committees, seized from the outset the control of the movement, and made it impossible for loyalty to show itself in concerted or effective action. And it is well known how numerous and active were the Tories in the Carolinas. But, says Dr. Ramsay, speaking of South Carolina, "Beside their superiority in numbers, there was an ardour and enthusiasm in the friends of Congress which was generally wanting in the advocates for royal government." Is not this a most significant touch? After all the evidence as to classes and numbers—for perhaps there were a hundred thousand Loyalist exiles, to say nothing of the many more who did not emigrate—the ultimate success of the American cause might well seem to us a miracle. But the fact remains that the Revolutionary party knew what they wanted. They had a definite programme, they had boldness and resolution, while those averse to independence were divided in their counsels, and paralyzed by the timidity which naturally cleaves to conservative minds. The first scientific observer of political revolutions, Thucydides, pointed out, and every subsequent revolution has accentuated his words, that in such times boldness and energy are more important requisites to success than intelligence or all other qualities put together. This is the secret of the whole matter. "There was an ardour and enthusiasm in the friends of Congress which was generally wanting in the advocates for royal government."

All things considered, it seems clear that in most states the strength of the revolutionary party lay most largely in the plain people, as distinguished from the aristocracy. It lay not in the mob or rabble, for American society was overwhelmingly rural and not urban, and had no sufficient amount of mob or rabble to control the movement, but in the peasantry, substantial and energetic though poor, in the small farmers and frontiersmen. And so, although there were men of great possessions like George Washington and Charles Carroll of Carrollton who contributed a conservative element, in the main we must expect to see our social changes tending in the direction of levelling democracy.

It would be aside from the declared purpose of these lectures to dwell upon the political effects which resulted from the victory of a party constituted in the manner that has been described. There are, however, some political changes that almost inevitably bring social changes in their wake. Take, for instance, the expansion of the suffrage. The status in which the electoral franchise was left at the end of the Revolutionary period fell far short of complete democracy. Yet during the years we are considering the right of suffrage was much extended. The freeholder, or owner of real estate, was given special privileges in four of the new state constitutions, two others widened the suffrage to include all owners of either land or personal property to a certain limit, and two others conferred it upon all tax-payers. Now if in this lecture we are considering especially the status of persons, we must take account of the fact that the elevation of whole classes of people to the status of voters elevates them also in their social status. American society in the colonial period had a more definite and stable organization than it ever has had since the Revolution. It had been like that English county society of which the poet speaks,

> Where Aylmer followed Aylmer at the hall,
> And Averill Averill at the rectory.

Now, multitudes of squires had been driven into exile or dethroned from their high position of dominance over the community. Multitudes of other Loyalists had been disfranchised, or impoverished by confiscations. Rip Van Winkle, whose sleep bridged just these years, found the atmosphere of his village radically altered. Jeremy Belknap of New Hampshire, writing in 1792, after remarking on the effect of the Revolution in calling the democratic power into action and repressing the aristocratic spirit, confesses that in the new state "the deficiency of persons qualified for the various departments in the Government has been much regretted, and by none more than by those few who know how public business ought to be conducted." In that entertaining Virginian autobiography, the *Life* of the Reverend Devereux Jarratt, after speaking of the habit in that writer's youth, among the plain people with whom he grew up, of regarding gentle-folk as beings of a superior order, he says in 1794:

> But I have lived to see a vast alteration in this respect and the contrary extreme prevail. In our high republican times there is more levelling than ought to be, consistent with good government. I have as little notion of oppression and tyranny as any man, but a due subordination is essentially requisite in every government. At present there is too little regard and reverence paid to magistrates and persons in public office; and whence do this regard and irreverence originate but from the notion and practice of levelling? An idea is held out to us that our present government and state are far superior to the former, when we were under the royal administration; but my age enables me to know that the people are not now by half so peacefully and quietly governed as formerly; nor are the laws, perhaps by the tenth part, so well executed. And yet I know the superiority of the present government. In theory it is certainly superior; but in practice it is not so. This can arise from nothing so much as from want of a proper distinction between the various orders of the people.

Similar voices come from North Carolina, where one stout conservative laments the "extension of that most delicate and important right [of suffrage] to every biped of the forest," and another declares that: "Anyone who has the least pretence to be a gentleman is suspected and borne down *per ignobile vulgus*—a set of men without reading, experience, or principle to govern them." In fact, the sense of social change pervaded the country. A writer in South Carolina says, quite in the spirit of these lectures, "There is nothing more common than to confound the terms of the American Revolution with those of the late American war. The American war is over, but this is far from being the case with the American revolution. On the contrary, nothing but the first act of the great drama is closed."

The workings of the popular sentiment in favor of equality may of course be plainly seen in the legislation abolishing rights of primogeniture and distributing more or less equally the estates of persons dying intestate, but this movement may perhaps be more conveniently considered in a lecture devoted to the Revolution and the Land. We might also expect the equalitarian or humane spirit to show itself in alterations of the laws respecting redemptioners or indented servants. Those laws, however, seem not to have been changed in the Revolutionary period. We may infer that the laws protecting the interests of such persons, a very numerous class in the years just preceding the Revolution, either were, or were deemed to be, adequate already for their humane purpose, and that the status of the indented, who after all had but a few years to serve and then would have all the rights of other poor people, was not regarded as seriously unsatisfactory.

A far more serious question, in any consideration of the effect of the American Revolution on the status of persons, is that of its influence on the institution of slavery, for at this time the contrast between American freedom and American slavery comes out, for the first time, with startling distinctness. It has often been asked: How could men who were engaged in a great and inspiring struggle for liberty fail to perceive the inconsistency between their professions and endeavors in that contest and their actions with respect to their bondmen? How could they fail to see the application of their doctrines respecting the rights of man to the black men who were held among them in bondage far more reprehensible than that to which they indignantly proclaimed themselves to have been subjected by the King of Great Britain?

At the time when the Revolution broke out there were about a half-million of slaves in the Thirteen Colonies, the figures probably running about as follows: 200,000 in Virginia, 100,000 in South Carolina, 70,000 or 80,000 each in Maryland and in North Carolina, 25,000 perhaps in New York, 10,000 in New Jersey, 6,000 in Pennsylvania, 6,000 in Connecticut, 5,000 in Massachusetts, 4,000 in Rhode Island. Slavery in the continental colonies at that time was no doubt less harsh than in the West Indies, and milder than it has been in many other countries and times. An English parson, preaching to a Virginian congregation in 1763, says: "I do you no more than justice in bearing witness, that in no part of the world were slaves ever better treated than, in general, they are in the colonies." But slavery is slavery, and already before the Revolution many hearts had been stirred against it. It is of course true that other influences than those of the American Revolution were abroad in the world at the same time which would surely work in some degree against the institution of human slavery. On the one hand Voltaire had raised a powerful, if at times a grating, voice in favor of a rational humanitarianism, and Rousseau had poured upon time-worn institutions the active solvent of abounding sentimentality. Quite at another extreme of human thought from them, Wesley and Whitefield had stirred the English nation into a warmth of religious feeling of which Methodism was only one result, and with it came a revived interest in all varieties of philanthropic endeavor.

There is no lack of evidence that, in the American world of that time, the analogy between freedom for whites and freedom for blacks was seen. If we are to select but one example of such evidence, the foremost place must surely be given to the striking language of Patrick Henry, used in 1773, when he was immersed in the struggle against Great Britain. It is found in a letter which he wrote to one who had sent him a copy of Anthony Benezet's book on slavery.

> Is it not amazing [he says] that at a time, when the rights of humanity are defined and understood with precision, in a country above all others fond of liberty, that in such an age and in such a country we find men professing a religion the most humane, mild, gentle and generous, adopting a principle as repugnant to humanity as it is inconsistent with the Bible and destructive to liberty? . . . Would anyone believe I am the master of slaves of my own purchase! I am drawn along by the general inconvenience of living here without them. I will not, I can not justify it. However culpable my conduct, I will so far pay my devoir to virtue, as to own the excellence and rectitude of her precepts, and lament my want of conformity to them. I believe a time will come when an opportunity will be offered to abolish this lamentable evil. Everything we can do is to improve it, if it happens in our day, if not, let us transmit to our descendants, together with our slaves, a pity for their unhappy lot, and an abhorrence of slavery. . . . It is a debt we owe to the purity of our religion, to show that it is at variance with that law which warrants slavery.

Along with many examples and expressions of individual opinion, we may note the organized efforts toward the removal or alleviation of slavery manifested in the creation of a whole group of societies for these purposes. The first anti-slavery society in this or any other country was formed on April 14, 1775, five days before the battle of Lexington, by a meeting at the Sun Tavern, on Second Street in Philadelphia. The members were mostly of the Society of Friends. The organization took the name of "The Society for the Relief of Free Negroes unlawfully held in Bondage." In the preamble of their constitution they point out that "loosing the bonds of wickedness and setting the oppressed free, is evidently a duty incumbent on all professors of Christianity, but more especially at a time when justice, liberty, and the laws of the land are the general topics among most ranks and stations of men." The New York "Society for Promoting the Manumission of Slaves" was organized in 1785, with John Jay for its first president. In 1788 a society similar to these two was founded in Delaware, and within four years there were other such in Rhode Island, Connecticut, New Jersey, Maryland, and Virginia, and local societies enough to make at least thirteen, mostly in the slave-holding states.

In actual results of the growing sentiment, we may note, first of all, the checking of the importation of slaves, and thus of the horrors of the trans-Atlantic slave trade. The Continental Congress of 1774 had been in session but a few days when they decreed an "American Association," or non-importation agreement, in which one section read: "That we will neither import nor purchase any slave imported after the first day of December next, after which we will wholly discontinue the slave trade, and will neither be concerned in it ourselves, nor will we hire our vessels nor sell our commodities or manufactures to those who are concerned in it"; and the evidence seems to be that the terms of this agreement were enforced throughout the war with little evasion.

States also acted. Four months before this, in July 1774, Rhode Island had passed a law to the effect that all slaves thereafter brought into the colony should be free. The influence under which it was passed may be seen from the preamble. "Whereas," it begins, "the inhabitants of America are generally engaged in the preservation of their own rights and liberties, among which that of personal freedom must be considered as the greatest, and as those who are desirous of enjoying all the advantages of liberty themselves should be willing to extend personal liberty to others," etc. A similar law was passed that same year in Connecticut. Delaware prohibited importation in 1776, Virginia in 1778, Maryland in 1783, South Carolina in 1787, for a term of years, and North Carolina, in 1786, imposed a larger duty on each negro imported.

Still further, the states in which slaves were few proceeded, directly as a consequence of the Revolutionary movement, to effect the immediate or gradual abolition of slavery itself. Vermont had never recognized its existence, but Vermont was not recognized as a state. Pennsylvania in 1780 provided for gradual abolition, by an act which declared that no negro born after that date should be held in any sort of bondage after he became twenty-eight years old, and that up to that time his service should be simply like that of an indented servant or apprentice. Now what says the preamble of this act? That when we consider our deliverance from the abhorrent condition to which Great Britain has tried to reduce us, we are called on to manifest the sincerity of our professions of freedom, and to give substantial proof of gratitude, by extending a portion of our freedom to others, who, though of a different color, are the work of the same Almighty hand. Evidently here also the leaven of the Revolution was working as a prime cause in this philanthropic endeavor.

The Superior Court of Massachusetts declared that slavery had been abolished in that state by the mere declaration of its constitution that "all men are born free and equal." In 1784 Connecticut and Rhode Island passed acts which gradually extinguished slavery. In other states, ameliorations of the law respecting slaves were effected even though the abolition of slavery could not be brought about. Thus in 1782 Virginia passed an act which provided that any owner might, by an instrument properly attested, freely manumit all his slaves, if he gave security that their maintenance should not become a public charge. It may seem but a slight thing, this law making private manumission easy where before it had been difficult. But it appears to have led in eight years to the freeing of more than ten thousand slaves, twice as great a number as were freed by reason of the Massachusetts constitution, and as many as there were in Rhode Island and Connecticut together when the war broke out.

That all was not done that might have been done for the removal or amelioration of slavery we cannot deny, nor that there was in many places a glaring contrast between the principles avowed by the men of the Revolution and their acts respecting slavery; yet very substantial progress was made, and that more was made in this period than in any other until a much later time may be taken as clear evidence of a pronounced influence of the Revolution upon the status of persons in the realm where that status stood most in need of amelioration.

Thus in many ways the successful struggle for the independence of the United States affected the character of American society by altering the status of persons. The freeing of the community led not unnaturally to the freeing of the individual; the raising of colonies to the position of independent states brought with it the promotion of many a man to a higher order in the scale of privilege or consequence. So far at any rate as this aspect of life in America is concerned, it is vain to think of the Revolution as solely a series of political or military events.

6.

DANIEL J. BOORSTIN

In the middle of the twentieth century, as historians viewed the deep social antagonisms that had upset political and social institutions throughout much of the rest of the world, the American Revolution appeared by contrast to have been an orderly, conservative affair. Although the Revolution had undoubtedly stimulated and accelerated social change, so had every other major war in American history. Indeed a history of the Second World War considered as a social movement might disclose more sweeping social changes within the United States in the 1940s than those that occurred in the American Revolution. Yet the Second World War was not, for the United States at least, a Revolution. The significance of the American Revolution, then, it seemed to many historians, lay not in social change and conflict but in consensus and continuity. One of the most perceptive comments on the conservatism of the Revolution was that of Daniel J. Boorstin in the Charles R. Walgren Lectures at the University of Chicago in 1952. In the complexity and sophistication of his argument, as compared with the analogous one of Friedrich Gentz, one may measure the increasing range and depth of historical understanding. (Reprinted from The Genius of American Politics, *Chicago: The University of Chicago Press, 1953, pp. 66-98, by permission of the publisher.)*

The American Revolution: Revolution without Dogma

We are accustomed to think of the Revolution as the great age of American political thought. It may therefore be something of a shock to realize that it did not produce in America a single important treatise on political theory. Men like Franklin and Jefferson, universal in their interests, active and spectacularly successful in developing institutions, were not fertile as political philosophers.

In the present chapter I shall offer some explanations of this fact and shall explore some of its significance for our later political life. I shall be trying to discover why, in the era of our Revolution, a political theory failed to be born. But my inquiry will not be entirely negative. I will seek those features of the Revolution, those positive ideas and attitudes, which actually have done much to reinforce our sense of "givenness."

We have been slow to see some of the more obvious and more important peculiarities of our Revolution because influential scholars on the subject have cast their story in the mold of the French Revolution of 1789. Some of our best historians have managed to empty our Revolution of much of its local flavor by exaggerating what it had in common with that distinctively European struggle. This they have done in two ways.

First, they have stressed the international character of the intellectual movement of which the French Revolution was a classic expression—the so-called "Enlightenment." They speak of it as a "climate of opinion" whose effects, like the barometric pressure, could no more be escaped in America than in Europe. As Carl Becker put it in his *Heavenly City of the Eighteenth-Century Philosophers*: "The Enlightenment . . . is not a peculiarly French but an international climate of opinion . . . and in the new world Jefferson, whose sensitized mind picked up and transmitted every novel vibration in the intellectual air, and Franklin of Philadelphia, printer and friend of the human race—these also, whatever national or individual characteristics they may have exhibited, were true children of the Enlightenment. The philosophical empire was an international domain of which France was but the mother country and Paris the capital."

Second, they have treated ours as only a particular species of the genus "Revolution"—of what should perhaps more properly be called *revolutio Europaensis*. Since the French Revolution has been made the model, from that European revolution historians have borrowed the vocabulary in which ours is discussed and the calendar by which it is clocked. "Thermidor," for example, is the name used in one of our best college textbooks to introduce its chapter on the federal Constitution.

It goes on:

> There comes a time in every revolutionary movement when the people become tired of agitation and long for peace and security. They then eliminate the radicals, trouble-makers and warmongers, and take measures to consolidate their government, hoping to secure what has already been gained through turmoil and suffering. *Thermidor* this time is called in leftist language, from the counter-revolution in France that overthrew Robespierre and ended the reign of terror. Thus, the establishment of Cromwell as Lord Protector was the Thermidor of the English Revolution in the seventeenth century; and the Stalin dictatorship and exile of Trotsky marks the Thermidor of the Russian Revolution. Every taking of the Bastille, it may be said, is inevitably followed by Thermidor, since human nature craves security, and the progress of a revolution must be stopped somewhere short of anarchy [Morison and Commager, *Growth of the American Republic* (3d ed.; New York, 1942), I, 277].

The effect of all this has been to emphasize—or rather exaggerate—the similarity of ours to all other modern revolutions.

In so doing, historians have exaggerated the significance of what is supposed to have been the ideology of the Revolution. Such an emphasis has had the further attraction to some "liberal" historians of seeming to put us in the main current of European history. It has never been quite clear to me why historians would not have found our revolution significant enough merely as a victory of constitutionalism.

I. Some Peculiarities of Our Revolution

The most obvious peculiarity of our American Revolution is that, in the modern European sense of the word, it was hardly a revolution at all. The Daughters of the American Revolution, who have been understandably sensitive on this subject, have always insisted in their literature that the American Revolution was no revolution but merely a colonial rebellion. The more I have looked into the subject, the more convinced I have become of the wisdom of their naïveté. "The social condition and the Constitution of the Americans are democratic," De Tocqueville observed about a hundred years ago. "But they have not had a democratic revolution." This fact is surely one of the most important of our history.

A number of historians (J. Franklin Jameson and Merrill Jensen, for example) have pointed out the ways in which a social revolution, including a redistribution of property, accompanied the American Revolution. These are facts which no student of the period should neglect. Yet it seems to me that these historians have by no means succeeded in showing that such changes were so basic and so far-reaching as actually in themselves to have established our national republican institutions. When we speak of the Revolution therefore, we are still fully justified in referring to something other than what Jameson's disciples mean by "the American Revolution as a social movement." If we consider the American Revolution in that sense, it would not be a great deal more notable than a number of other social movements in our history, such as Jacksonianism, populism, progressivism, and the New Deal. Moreover, in so far as the American Revolution was a social movement, it was not much to be distinguished from European revolutions; and the increasing emphasis on this aspect of our history is but another example of the attempt to assimilate our history to that of Europe.

The Revolution, as the birthday of our nation, must mean something very different from all this. It is the series of events by which we separated ourselves from the British Empire and acquired a national identity. Looking at our Revolution from this point of view, what are some features which distinguish it from the French Revolution of 1789 or the other revolutions to which western

European nations trace their national identity? And, especially, what are those peculiarities which have affected the place of theory in our political life?

1. First, and most important, the United States was born in a *colonial* rebellion. Our national birth certificate is a Declaration of Independence and not a Declaration of the Rights of Man. The vast significance of this simple fact is too often forgotten. Compared even with other colonial rebellions, the American Revolution is notably lacking in cultural self-consciousness and in any passion for national unity. The more familiar type of colonial rebellion—like that which recently occurred in India—is one in which a subject people vindicates its local culture against foreign rulers. But the American Revolution had very little of this character. On the contrary, ours was one of the few conservative colonial rebellions of modern times.

We should recall several of the peculiar circumstances (most of them obvious) which had made this kind of revolution possible. At the time of the Revolution, the major part of the population of the American colonies was of British stock. Therefore, no plausible racial or national argument could be found for the superiority either of the inhabitants of the mother-country or of the continental American colonies. Even when Jefferson, in his *Notes on Virginia,* went to some trouble to refute Buffon and the Abbé Raynal and others who had argued that all races, including man, deteriorated on the American continent, he did not go so far as to say that the American races were distinctly superior.

Since the climate and topography of substantial parts of the American colonies were similar to those of the mother-country (and for a number of other reasons), there had been a pretty wholesale transplantation of British legal and political institutions to North America. Unlike the Spanish colonies in South America, which were to rebel, at least in part, because they had had so little home rule, the British colonies in North America were to rebel because, among other reasons, they had had so much. Finally, the North American continent was (except for sparse Indian settlements) empty of indigenous populations, hence barren of such local institutions and traditions as could have competed with what the colonists had brought with them.

All these facts were to make it easy, then, for the American Revolution to seem in the minds of most of its leaders an affirmation of the tradition of British institutions. The argument of the best theorists of the Revolution—perhaps we should call them lawyers rather than theorists—was not, on the whole, that America had institutions or a culture superior to that of the British. Rather their position, often misrepresented and sometimes simply forgotten, was that the British by their treatment of the American colonies were being untrue to the ancient spirit of their own institutions. The slogan "Taxation without Representation Is Tyranny" was clearly founded on a British assumption. As James Otis put it in his pamphlet, *The Rights of the British Colonies* (1764), he believed "that this [British] constitution is the most free one, and by far the best, now existing on earth: that by this constitution, every man in the dominions is a free man: that no parts of His Majesty's dominions can be taxed without their consent: that every part has a right to be represented in the supreme or some subordinate legislature: that the refusal of this would seem to be a contradiction in practice to the theory of the constitution."

According to their own account, then, the Americans were to have forced on them the need to defend the ancient British tradition; to be truer to the spirit of that tradition than George III and Lord North and Townshend knew how to be. They were fighting not so much to establish new rights as to preserve old ones: "for the preservation of our liberties . . . in defence of the freedom that is our birthright, and which we ever enjoyed till the late violation of it" (Declaration of Causes of Taking up Arms, July 6, 1775). From the colonists' point of view, until 1776 it was Parliament that had been revolutionary, by exercising a power for which there was no warrant in English constitutional precedent. The ablest defender of the Revolution—in fact, the greatest political theorist of the American Revolution—was also the great theorist of British conservatism, Edmund Burke.

2. Second, the American Revolution was *not* the product of a nationalistic spirit. We had no Bismarck or Cavour or any nationalist philosophy. We were singularly free from most of the philosophical baggage of modern nationalism.

Perhaps never was a new nation created with less enthusiasm. To read the history of our Revolution is to discover that the United

States was a kind of *pis aller*. This fact explains many of the difficulties encountered in conducting the Revolution and in framing a federal constitution. The original creation of a United States was the work of doubly reluctant men: men reluctant, both because of their local loyalties—to Virginia, Massachusetts, Rhode Island, and New York—and because of their imperial loyalty. The story of the "critical period" of American history, of the Articles of Confederation and the Constitution, tells of the gradual overcoming of this reluctance. It was overcome not by any widespread conversion to a nationalist theory—even the *Federalist* papers are conspicuously lacking in such a theory—but by gradual realization of the need for effective union.

In the period of the American Revolution we do discover a number of enthusiasms: for the safety and prosperity of Virginia or New York, for the cause of justice, for the rights of Englishmen. What is missing is anything that might be called widespread enthusiasm for the birth of a new nation: the United States of America. Until well into the nineteenth century, Jefferson—and he was not alone in this—was using the phrase "my country" to refer to his native state of Virginia.

3. Our Revolution was successful at the first try. This is equally true whether we consider it as a revolt against British rule or as a movement for republican federalism. There was no long-drawn-out agitation, no intellectual war of attrition, of the sort which breeds dogmas and intransigence. Thomas Paine's *Common Sense,* which is generally considered "the first important republican tract to be issued in America . . . the first to present cogent arguments for independence," did not appear until January 10, 1776. Down to within six months of the break, few would have considered independence; and even then the colonists had only quite specific complaints. There had been no considerable tradition in America either of revolt against British institutions or of republican theorizing.

The political objective of the Revolution, independence from British rule, was achieved by one relatively short continuous effort. More commonly in modern history (take, for example, the European revolutions of the nineteenth century) any particular revolt has been only one in a long series. Each episode, then, ends on a note of suspense which comes from the feeling that the story is "to be continued." Under those circumstances, challenges to constituted authority follow one another, accumulating their ideological baggage.

In France, for example, 1789 was followed by 1830 and 1848 and 1870; a similar list could be made for Italy, Germany, and perhaps Russia. Such repetition creates a distinctive revolutionary tradition, with continued agitation keeping alive certain doctrines. Repeated efforts provide the dogmatic raw material for a profusion of later political parties, each of which rallies under the banner of one or another of the defeated revolutions or of a revolution yet to be made. But, properly speaking, 1776 had no sequel, and needed none. The issue was separation, and separation was accomplished.

II. How We Have Been Led To Ignore These Peculiarities

The student who comes for the first time to the literature of our Revolution is liable to be disappointed by the dull and legalistic flavor of what he has to read. Although the American Revolution occurred in an age which throughout Europe was laden with philosophic reflection and important treatises, our Revolution was neither particularly rich nor particularly original in its intellectual apparatus. The documents of that era, as Moses Coit Tyler described them, are "a vast morass of technical discussion, into which, perhaps, no living reader will ever follow the writer, from which, in fact, the writer himself never emerges alive."

Orators, textbook-writers, and other tradition-makers have been hard put to it to find those ringing phrases, the battle-cries and philosophical catchwords, which slip smoothly off the tongue, remain fixed in the memory, and uplift the soul. This helps explain why a few phrases and documents have been overworked and why even these have always been read only in part or out of context. The first two paragraphs of the Declaration of Independence have been worn thin; few bother to read the remaining thirty. People have grasped at "life, liberty, and the pursuit of happiness," forgetting that it was two-thirds borrowed and, altogether, only part of a preamble. We have repeated that "all men are created equal," without daring to discover what it meant and without realizing that probably to none of the men who spoke it did it mean what we would like it to mean. Or we have exploited passages in the "speeches" of Patrick Henry, which were actually composed less by Henry than by his biographers.

The proper slogan of the Revolution—if, indeed, there was a slogan—was "No Taxation without Representation." Such words are far too polysyllabic, far too legalistic, to warm the popular heart. But if we compare them with the "Liberty, Equality, Fraternity" of the French Revolution and the "Peace, Bread, and Land," of the Russian, we have a clue to the peculiar spirit of the American Revolution. It is my view that the major issue of the American Revolution was the true constitution of the British Empire, which is a pretty technical legal problem. This notion is supported by Professor Charles H. McIlwain, who, in his admirable little book on the American Revolution, comes closer than any other recent historian to the spirit of our Revolutionary age.

In that age men were inclined to take their opponents at their word; the Revolutionary debate seems to have been carried on in the belief that men meant what they said. But in this age of Marx and Freud we have begun to take it for granted that, if people talk about one thing, they must be thinking about something else. Ideas are treated as the apparatus of an intellectual sleight-of-hand, by which the speaker diverts the audience's attention to an irrelevant subject while he does the real business unobserved. To study the Revolutionary debate is then to try to see (in the phrase of one historian) how "the colonists modified their theory to suit their needs." From such a point of view, there is perhaps never much political or legal thought worth talking about; to be realistic we should focus our discussion on hormones and statistics.

But such an approach would bleach away the peculiar tone of our history and empty our Revolution of its unique significance. Therefore, even at the risk of seeming naïve, I should like to consider the outlandish possibility that men like Jefferson and Adams all along meant what they were saying, that is, that the Revolution had something to do with the British constitution.

First, however, I should like briefly to describe the interpretation which in recent decades has had increasing vogue. That interpretation has taken two forms, both of which minimize the significance of the constitutional debate. Both views are instrumentalist and cosmopolitan in their emphasis: one starts from the history of ideas, and the other from economic history. The first of these is the point of view which was popularized by the late Carl Becker, who helped create the mold in which American accounts of the Revolution have been cast for the last several decades. According to this view, the colonists *began* their argument on a low legalistic level, finding it convenient to debate first within the framework of the imperial constitution and the common law; but they gradually and inevitably climbed the ladder of abstraction until, by mid-1776, they were thinking and talking in the arid heights of natural law.

"When the controversy with Great Britain began in 1764," Carl Becker writes in his influential book, *The Declaration of Independence,* "the preconceptions of the Natural Rights philosophy lay quiescent in colonial minds, ready to be drawn upon in case of need, but never yet having been called forth in the service of any concrete issue." Becker draws the lines from Locke and Newton forward to Franklin, Jefferson, and Adams, and he describes the several stages in the argument:

> Thus step by step, from 1764 to 1776, the colonists modified their theory to suit their needs. They were not altogether unaware of the fact. . . . Profoundly convinced that they deserved to be free, Americans were primarily concerned with the moral or rational basis of their claims. . . . "If these now so considerable places are not represented, they ought to be." . . . But the "ought to be" is not ultimately to be found in positive law and custom. . . . Whenever men become sufficiently dissatisfied with what is, with the existing regime of positive law and custom, they will be found reaching out beyond it for the rational basis of what they conceive ought to be. This is what the Americans did in their controversy with Great Britain; and this rational basis they found in that underlying preconception which shaped the thought of their age—the idea of natural law and natural rights [(New York, 1933), pp. 133 f.].

By the time the Revolution became a fact, Americans were supposedly speaking the language of French philosophers. As they became more and more revolutionary, their argument, it is suggested, became less and less American.

A close reading of Becker reveals that he draws his evidence of the popularity of natural-law thinking more from English and

French than from American sources. He does not offer us convincing examples of the adoption of Newtonian thinking into the writings of the American Revolutionary theorists. But, however this may be, any such interpretation is possible only if one projects back into the age of Jefferson a kind of skepticism about the common law and about the existence of rights themselves which was foreign to that age as a whole, and was especially antipathetic to our Revolutionary leaders.

The conventional account which we have been describing rests on an assumption that the colonists were engaged primarily—if not exclusively—in rationalizing their dissatisfactions. At the very least, it supposes a kind of intellectual mobility—near disingenuousness—which enabled the Americans to shift their ground to suit their needs. It takes for granted that colonial statements were mere polemics and therefore that the colonists could as readily abandon the legal for the philosophical level of argument as a hired counsel could alter his plea from guilty to not guilty. It overlooks certain obvious possibilities: that, all along, the colonists were saying what they really believed; that their loyalty to British institutions was itself a cause of the Revolution; and that therefore their enthusiasm for those institutions could not be put aside like a lawyer's brief.

The second form of the modern interpretation has been rooted in a similarly cosmopolitan and instrumentalist frame of mind. This views our history not so much in the realm of general ideas as in the perspective of world economic development. Perhaps, it is suggested, the Revolution might better be seen as merely an episode in the growth of modern capitalism. The books of Charles A. Beard gave some support to this way of thinking. As Louis Hacker puts it in his *Triumph of American Capitalism*:

> The struggle was not over high-sounding political and constitutional concepts: over the power of taxation or even, in the final analysis, over natural rights. It was over colonial manufacturing, wild lands and furs, sugar, wine, tea, and currency, all of which meant, simply, the survival or collapse of English mercantile capitalism within the imperial-colonial framework of the mercantilist system [(New York, 1940), p. 161].

If the real motives were economic, the true purposes of the Revolutionaries lie hidden in financial archives, and what they said was actually not too important. The Revolutionary debate was only a frontier skirmish in the world-wide struggle for modern capitalism.

III. The Conservatism of the Revolution

In order convincingly to refute either of these current views it would be necessary to retell the whole story of the Revolution. Obviously, this is not the place for such a narrative. My purpose here is rather to emphasize a certain aspect of the Revolution which in my opinion has not been given the emphasis it deserves. As new facts have been discovered and new interpretations manufactured, our historians have not readily added these new interpretations to the old, in order to produce a more complex and therefore perhaps a more valid explanation of a complex event. Rather they have been inclined to discard the wisdom of an older emphasis for that of a new. Hence it is that one of the more obvious aspects of the Revolution has been increasingly neglected.

The feature to which I want to direct your attention might be called the "conservatism" of the Revolution. If we understand this characteristic, we will begin to see the Revolution as an illustration of the remarkable continuity of American history. And we will also see how the attitude of our Revolutionary thinkers has engraved more deeply in our national consciousness a belief in the inevitability of our particular institutions, or, in a word, our sense of "givenness."

The character of our Revolution has nourished our assumption that whatever institutions we happened to have here (in this case the British constitution) had the self-evident validity of anything that is "normal." We have thus casually established the tradition that it is superfluous to the American condition to produce elaborate treatises on political philosophy or to be explicit about political values and the theory of community.

I shall confine myself to two topics. First, the manifesto of the Revolution, namely, the Declaration of Independence; and, second, the man who has been generally considered the most outspoken and systematic political philosopher of the Revolution, Thomas Jefferson. Of course, I will not try to give a full account of either of them. I will attempt only to call your attention to a few facts which may not have been sufficiently emphasized and which are especially significant for our present purpose. Obviously, no one could contend that there is either in the man or in the document nothing of the cosmopolitan spirit, nothing of the world climate of opinion. My suggestion is simply that we do find another spirit of at least equal, and perhaps overshadowing, importance and that this spirit may actually be more characteristic of our Revolution.

First, then, for the Declaration of Independence. Its technical, legalistic, and conservative character, which I wish to emphasize, will appear at once by contrast with the comparable document of the French Revolution. Ours was concerned with a specific event, namely, the separation of these colonies from the mother-country. But the French produced a "Declaration of the Rights of *Man* and the Citizen." When De Tocqueville, in his *Ancien Régime* (Book I, chap. iii), sums up the spirit of the French Revolution, he is describing exactly what the American Revolution was not:

> The French Revolution acted, with regard to things of this world, precisely as religious revolutions have acted with regard to things of the other. It dealt with the citizen in the abstract, independent of particular social organizations, just as religions deal with mankind in general, independent of time and place. It inquired, not what were the particular rights of the French citizens, but what were the general rights and duties of mankind in reference to political concerns.
>
> It was by thus divesting itself of all that was peculiar to one race or time, and by reverting to natural principles of social order and government, that it became intelligible to all, and susceptible of simultaneous imitation in a hundred different places.
>
> By seeming to tend rather to the regeneration of the human race than to the reform of France alone, it roused passions such as the most violent political revolutions had been incapable of awakening. It inspired proselytism, and gave birth to propagandism; and hence assumed that quasi religious character which so terrified those who saw it, or, rather, became a sort of new religion, imperfect, it is true, without God, worship, or future life, but still able, like Islamism, to cover the earth with its soldiers, its apostles, and its martyrs [trans. John Bonner (New York, 1856), pp. 26 f.].

In contrast to all this, our Declaration of Independence is essentially a list of specific historical instances. It is directed not to the regeneration but only to the "opinions" of mankind. It is closely tied to time and place; the special affection for "British brethren" is freely admitted; it is concerned with the duties of a particular king and certain of his subjects.

Even if we took only the first two paragraphs or preamble, which are the most general part of the document, and actually read them as a whole, we could make a good case for their being merely a succinct restatement of the Whig theory of the British revolution of 1688. Carl Becker himself could not overlook this fact. "In political theory and in political practice," he wrote parenthetically, "the American Revolution drew its inspiration from the parliamentary struggle of the seventeenth century. The philosophy of the Declaration was not taken from the French. It was not even new; but good old English doctrine newly formulated to meet a present emergency." To be understood, its words must be annotated by British history. This is among the facts which have led some historians (Guizot, for example) to go so far as to say that the English revolution succeeded twice, once in England and once in America.

The remaining three-quarters—the unread three-quarters—of the document is technical and legalistic. That is, of course, the main reason why it remains unread. For it is a bill of indictment against the king, written in the language of British constitutionalism. "The patient sufferance of these Colonies" is the point of departure. It deals with rights and franchises under British charters. It carefully recounts that the customary and traditional forms of protest, such as "repeated Petitions," have already been tried.

The more the Declaration is reread in context, the more plainly it appears a document of imperial legal relations rather than a piece of high-flown political philosophy. The desire to remain true to the principles of British constitutionalism up to the bitter end explains why, as has been often remarked, the document is directed against the king, despite the fact that the practical grievances were against Parliament; perhaps also why at this stage there is no longer an explicit appeal to the rights of Englishmen. Most of the document is a bald enumeration of George III's failures, excesses, and crimes in violation of the constitution and laws of Great Britain. One indictment after another makes sense only if one presupposes the framework of British constitutionalism. How else, for example, could one indict a king "for depriving us in many cases, of the benefits of Trial by Jury"?

We can learn a great deal about the context of our Revolutionary thought by examining Jefferson's own thinking down to the period of the Revolution. We need not stretch a point or give Jefferson a charismatic role, to say that the flavor of his thought is especially important for our purposes. He has been widely considered the leading political philosopher of the Revolution. Among other things, he was, of course, the principal author of the Declaration of Independence itself; and the Declaration has been taken to be the climax of the abstract philosophizing of the revolutionaries. Because he is supposed to be the avant-garde of revolutionary thought, evidence of conservatism and legalism in Jefferson's thought as a whole is especially significant.

We now are beginning to have a definitive edition of Jefferson's papers (edited by Julian P. Boyd and published by the Princeton University Press), which is one of the richest treasures ever amassed for the historian of a particular period. This helps us use Jefferson's thought as a touchstone. Neither in the letters which Jefferson wrote nor in those he received do we discover that he and his close associates—at least down to the date of the Revolution—showed any conspicuous interest in political theory. We look in vain for general reflections on the nature of government or constitutions. The manners of the day did require that a cultivated gentleman be acquainted with certain classics of political thought; yet we lack evidence that such works were read with more than a perfunctory interest. To be sure, when Jefferson prepares a list of worthy books for a young friend in 1771, he includes references to Montesquieu, Sidney, and Bolingbroke; but such references are rare. Even when he exchanges letters with Edmund Pendleton on the more general problems of institutions, he remains on the level of legality and policy, hardly touching political theory. Jefferson's papers for the Revolutionary period (read without the hindsight which has put the American and the French revolutions in the same era of world history) show little evidence that the American Revolution was a goad to higher levels of abstract thinking about society. We miss any such tendency in what Jefferson and his associates were reading or in what they were writing.

On the other hand, we find ample evidence that the locale of early Jeffersonian thought was distinctly *colonial;* we might even say *provincial.* And we begin to see some of the significance of that fact in marking the limits of political theorizing in America. By 1776, when the irreversible step of revolution was taken, the colonial period in the life of Jefferson and the other Revolutionary thinkers was technically at an end; but by then their minds had been congealed, their formal education completed, their social habits and the cast of their political thinking determined. The Virginia society of the pre-Revolutionary years had been decidedly derivative, not only in its culture, its furniture, its clothes, and its books, but in many of its ideas and—what is more to our purpose—in perhaps most of its institutions.

It is an important and little-noted fact that for many American thinkers of the period (including Jefferson himself) the cosmopolitan period in their thought did not begin until several years *after* their Revolution. Then, as representatives of the new nation, some of them were to enter the labyrinth of European diplomacy. Much of what we read of their experiences abroad even in this later period would confirm our impression of their naïveté, their strangeness to the sophisticated Paris of Talleyrand, the world of the *philosophes*. In Jefferson's particular case, the cosmopolitan period of his thought probably did not begin much before his first trip abroad as emissary to France in 1784.

When John Adams had gone, also to France, a few years earlier on his first foreign mission, he thought himself fresh from an "American Wilderness." Still more dramatic is the unhappy career of John Marshall, who was an innocent abroad if there ever was one. The career of Franklin, who was at least two generations older than these Revolutionary leaders, is something of an exception; but even in his case much of his charm for the salons of Paris consisted in his successful affectation of the character of a frontiersman.

The importance of this colonial framework in America, as I have already suggested, was to be enormous, not only from the point of view of Revolutionary thought, but in its long-run effect on the role of political theory in American life. The legal institutions which Americans considered their own and which they felt bound to master were largely borrowed. Jefferson and John Adams, both lawyers by profession, like their English contemporaries, had extracted much of their legal knowledge out of the crabbed pages of Coke's *Institutes*.

Now there were the elegant lectures of Sir William Blackstone, published as the four-volume *Commentaries on the Laws of England,* appearing between 1765 and 1769. It was this work of the ultra-conservative interpreter of English law that for many years remained the bible of American lawyers and, for several generations of them, virtually their whole bookish education. Blackstone's *Commentaries,* as Burke remarked in his Speech on Conciliation, had even by 1775 sold nearly as many copies in America as in England. American editions were numerous and popular; despite copious emendations and contradicting footnotes, Blackstone's original framework was faithfully preserved. Lincoln (as Carl Sandburg describes him), sitting barefoot on a woodpile in Illinois, fifty years later, reading the volumes of the conservative English lawyer—which he called the foundation of his own legal education—is a symbol of that continuity which has characterized our thinking about institutions. For our present purposes, the significant fact is that such a work as the *Commentaries* and the institutions which it expounded could continue to dominate the legal thinking of a people who were rebelling against the country of its origin.

During the very years when the Revolution was brewing, Jefferson was every day talking the language of the common law. We cannot but be impressed not only, as I have remarked, at the scarcity in the Jefferson papers for these years of anything that could be called fresh inquiry into the theory of government but also by the legalistic context of Jefferson's thought. We begin to see that the United States was being born in an atmosphere of legal rather than philosophical debate. Even apart from those technical legal materials with which Jefferson earned his living, his political pieces themselves possess a legal rather than a philosophical flavor.

A Summary View of the Rights of British America (July, 1774), which first brought Jefferson wide notice and which was largely responsible for his momentous choice on the committee to draft a declaration of independence, is less a piece of political theory than a closely reasoned legal document. He justifies the American position by appeal to the Saxon precedent: "No circumstance has occurred to distinguish materially the British from the Saxon emigration." It was from this parallel of the Americans with the Saxons, who also had once conquered a wilderness, that Jefferson draws several important legal consequences.

Jefferson's draft of the "new" Virginia Constitution of 1776 reveals a similar legalistic spirit: his Preamble comprised no premises of government in general, but only the same specific indictments of George III which were to be the substance of the Declaration of Independence. Jefferson actually describes the powers of the chief administrator as, with certain exceptions, "the powers formerly held by the king."

Jefferson's solid achievements in the period up to the Revolution were thus mainly works of legal draftsmanship. The reputation which he first obtained by his *Summary View,* he was to substantiate by other basic documents like the Virginia Constitution and by a host of complex public bills like those for dividing the county of Fincastle, for disestablishing the Church of England, for the naturalization of foreigners, and for the auditing of public accounts. Jefferson was equally at home in the intricacies of real-property law and in the problems of criminal jurisdiction. One of the many consequences of the neglect of American legal history has been our failure to recognize the importance of this legal element in our Revolutionary tradition. Jefferson's chef d'œuvre, a most impressive technical performance, was his series of Bills for Establishing Courts of Justice in Virginia. These bills, apparently drafted within about ten days in late 1776, show a professional virtuosity which any lawyer would envy.

The striking feature of these lawyerly accomplishments to those of us fed on clichés about the Age of Reason is how they live and move and have their being in the world of the common law, in the world of estates tail, bills in chancery, writs of supersedeas, etc., and not in the plastic universe of an eighteenth-century *philosophe.* Our evidence is doubly convincing, for the very reason that Jefferson was something of a reformer in legal matters. Yet even in his extensive projects of reform, he was eager to build on the foundation of the common law; for example, in his plan for the reform of the law of crimes and punishments. His tenacious conservatism appears in bold relief when we remind ourselves that Jefferson was a contemporary of Bentham, whose first important work, the *Fragment on Government,* also appeared in 1776.

But Jefferson did not found his reforms on any metaphysical calculus—rather on legal history and a continuity with the past. Even when he opposed feudal land tenures, he sought support from British sources. In the *Summary View* he had noted that feudal tenures were unknown to "our Saxon ancestors." "Has not every restitution of the antient Saxon laws had happy effects?" To have preserved the feudal tenures would actually have been, in Jefferson's words, "against the practice of our wise British ancestors. . . . Have not instances in which we have departed from this in Virginia been constantly condemned by the universal voice of our country?" (August 13, 1776; *Papers,* ed. Julian P. Boyd [Princeton, 1950], I, 492). Jefferson asked: "Is it not better now that we return at once into that happy system of our ancestors, the wisest and most perfect ever yet devised by the wit of man, as it stood before the 8th century?"

It is worth noting that Jefferson, who was to be the principal political philosopher of the Revolution, was given leadership in the important technical project of legal codification and reform in his native state of Virginia. Had he died at the end of 1776, he would probably have been remembered as a promising young lawyer of reformist bent, especially talented as a legal draftsman. In both houses of the Virginia legislature he had received the highest number of ballots in the election of members of the committee of legal revisers. The gist of the report of that committee (which included Edmund Pendleton, George Wythe, and George Mason, three of the ablest legal scholars on the continent, all active in the Revolution) is significant for our purposes. Jefferson himself recalled some years later that the commission had determined "not to meddle with the common law, i.e., the law preceding the existence of the statutes, further than to accommodate it to our new principles and circumstances."

Jefferson's philosophic concern with politics by the outbreak of the Revolution (actually only the end of his thirty-third year) was the enthusiasm of a reflective and progressive colonial lawyer for the traditional rights of Englishmen. To be sure, Jefferson did go further than some of his fellow-lawyers in his desire for legal reform —of feudal tenures, of entails, of the law of inheritance, of criminal law, and of established religion—yet even these projects were not, at least at that time, part of a coherent theory of society. They remained discrete reforms, "improvements" on the common law.

Jefferson's willingness to devote himself to purification of the common law must have rested on his faith in those ancient institutions and a desire to return to their essentials. This faith shines through those general maxims and mottoes about government which men took seriously in the eighteenth century and which often imply much more than they say. Jefferson's personal motto, "Rebellion to Tyrants Is Obedience to God," expresses pretty much the sum of his political theory—if, indeed, we should call it a "theory"—in this epoch. It was this motto (which Jefferson probably borrowed from Franklin, who offered it in 1776 for the Seal of the United States) that Jefferson himself proposed for Virginia and which he used on the seal for his own letters. But when we try to discover the meaning of the slogan to Jefferson, we find that it must be defined by reference less to any precise theology than to certain clear convictions about the British constitution. For who, after all, was a "tyrant"? None other than one who violated the sacred tenets of the ancient common law. Jefferson made his own view clear in the device which he suggested for the obverse of the United States seal: figures of "Hengist and Horsa, the Saxon chiefs from whom we claim the honor of being descended, and whose political principles and form of government we have assumed" (quoted by John Adams to Mrs. Adams, August 14, 1776; *Familiar Letters* [New York, 1875], p. 211).

In the Revolutionary period, when the temptations to be dogmatic were greatest, Jefferson did not succumb. The awareness of the peculiarity of America had not yet by any means led Jefferson to a rash desire to remake all society and institutions. What we actually discern is a growing tension between his feeling of the novelty of the American experience, on the one hand, and his feeling of belonging to ancient British institutions, on the other.

The tension was admirably expressed in Du Simitière's design for a coat of arms for Virginia. How large a hand Jefferson, who seems to have counseled Du Simitière, had in inventing the design is actually uncertain. But, regardless of authorship, the design eloquently portrays—indeed, almost caricatures—the current attitude. The indigenous glories of the New World were represented on the four quarters of the shield by a tobacco plant, two wheat sheafs, "a stalk of Indian corn full ripe," and "four fasces . . . alluding to the four gr[e]at rivers of Virginia." The background, the supporting and decorative elements—in fact, all parts of the arms that have any reference to institutions—emphasize the continuity of the British tradition. This was in August, 1776, after the date of the Declaration of Independence.

> Field a cross of St. george gules (as a remnant of the ancient coat of arms [showing] the origin of the Virginians to be English). . . . Supporters Dexter a figure dressed as in the time of Queen Elizabeth representing Sir Walter Rawleigh planting with his right hand the standard of liberty with the words MAGNA CHARTA written on it, with his left supporting the shield, Senester a Virginian rifle man of the present times compleatly accoutr[ed.]
>
> Crest. the crest of the antient arms of Virginia, the bust of a virgin naked and crowned with an antique crown. alluding to the Queen Elizabeth in whose reign the country was discover'd.
>
> Motto. "Rebellion to Tyrants is Obedience to God," or "Rex est qui regem non habet" [*Papers,* I, 510 ff.].

It would be possible to multiply examples of the importance of the continuing legal framework in the thought of other leaders of the Revolution. Few would be more interesting than John Adams, another of the authors of the Declaration of Independence. During the Revolutionary era, he elaborated a theory of the British Empire and developed in detail the notion of an unconstitutional act. His thought in this era has been characterized by Randolph G. Adams as that of a "Britannic Statesman."

IV. Revolution without Dogma: A Legacy of Institutions

We begin to see how far we would be misled, were we to cast American events of this era in the mold of European history. The American Revolution was in a very special way conceived as both a vindication of the British past and an affirmation of an American future. The British past was contained in ancient and living institutions rather than in doctrines; and the American future was never to be contained in a theory. The Revolution was thus a prudential decision taken by men of principle rather than the affirmation of a theory. What British institutions meant did not need to be articulated; what America might mean was still to be discovered.

This continuity of American history was to make a sense of "givenness" easier to develop; for it was this continuity which had made a new ideology of revolution seem unnecessary.

Perhaps the intellectual energy which American Revolutionaries economized because they were not obliged to construct a whole theory of institutions was to strengthen them for their encounter with nature and for their solution of practical problems. The effort which Jefferson, for example, did not care to spend on the theory of sovereignty he was to give freely to the revision of the criminal law, the observation of the weather, the mapping of the continent, the collection of fossils, the study of Indian languages, and the doubling of the national area.

The experience of our Revolution may suggest that the sparseness of American political theory, which has sometimes been described as a refusal of American statesmen to confront their basic philosophical problems, has been due less to a conscious refusal than to a simple lack of necessity. As the British colonists in America had forced on them the need to create a nation, so they had forced on them the need to be traditional and empirical in their institutions. The Revolution, because it was conceived as essentially affirming the British constitution, did not create the kind of theoretical vacuum made by some other revolutions.

The colonial situation, it would seem, had provided a *ne plus ultra* beyond which political theorizing did not need to range. Even Jefferson, the greatest and most influential theorist of the Revolution, remained loath to trespass that boundary, except under pressure: the pressure of a need to create a new federal structure. Mainly in the realm of federalism were new expedients called for. And no part of our history is more familiar than the story of how the framers of the federal Constitution achieved a solution: by compromise on details rather than by agreement on a theory.

There is hardly better evidence of this fact than the character of *The Federalist* papers themselves. Nearly everything about them illustrates or even symbolizes the way of political thinking which I have tried to describe. *The Federalist or, The New Constitution* consists of essays written by Alexander Hamilton, James Madison, and John Jay and published one at a time in certain New York journals between late 1787 and early 1788. They had a simple practical purpose: to persuade the people of the state of New York to ratify the recently drawn federal Constitution. The eighty-five numbers were written, like any series of newspaper articles, to be read separately, each essay being a unit. Their object is summarized by Hamilton in No. 1:

> I propose, in a series of papers, to discuss the following interesting particulars:—The utility of the UNION to your political prosperity—The insufficiency of the present Confederation to preserve that Union—The necessity of a government at least equally energetic with the one proposed, to the attainment of this object—The conformity of the proposed Constitution to the true principles of republican government—Its analogy to your own State constitution—and lastly, The additional security which its adoption will afford to the preservation of that species of government, to liberty, and to property.

If, indeed, *The Federalist* may be considered a treatise on political theory, it differs from other important works of the kind, by being an argument in favor of a particular written constitution. In this it is sharply distinguished from the writings of Plato, Aristotle, Hobbes, Locke, Rousseau, and J. S. Mill, which give us either systematic theories of the state or wide-ranging speculation. The organization of *The Federalist* papers is practical rather than systematic: they proceed from the actual dangers which confronted Americans to the weaknesses of the existing confederation and the specific advantages of the various provisions of the new constitution.

While the individual essays are full of wisdom, we must not forget, as Sir William Ashley reminds us, that "*The Federalist* has come to stand out more distinctly in the public view because of the oblivion that has befallen the torrent of other controversial writings of the same period." *The Federalist* essays are too often treated as if they comprised a single logical structure. They were a collaborative work mainly in the sense that their authors agreed on the importance of adopting the new constitution, not in the sense that the authors start from common and explicit philosophic premises. Hamilton, Madison, and Jay differed widely in personality and in philosophic position: individually they had even favored some other institutions than those embodied in the Constitution. But they had accepted the compromises and were convinced that what was being offered was far superior to what they already had. To read *The Federalist* is to discover the wisdom of Calhoun's observation that "this admirable federal constitution of ours . . . is superior to the wisdom of any or all of the men by whose agency it was made. The force of circumstances, and not foresight or wisdom, induced them to adopt many of its wisest provisions" (*Works,* ed. R. K. Cralle [New York, 1888], IV, 417).

The Revolution itself, as we have seen, had been a kind of affirmation of faith in ancient British institutions. In the greater part of the institutional life of the community the Revolution thus required no basic change. If any of this helps to illustrate or explain our characteristic lack of interest in political philosophy, it also helps to account for the value which we still attach to our inheritance from the British constitution: trial by jury, due process of law, representation before taxation, habeas corpus, freedom from attainder, independence of the judiciary, and the rights of free speech, free petition, and free assembly, as well as our narrow definition of treason and our antipathy to standing armies in peacetime. It also explains our continuing—sometimes bizarre, but usually fortunate—readiness to think of these traditional rights of Englishmen as if they were indigenous to our continent. In the proceedings of the San Francisco Vigilance Committee of 1851, we hear crude adventurers on the western frontier describing the technicalities of habeas corpus as if they were fruits of the American environment, as natural as human equality.

7.

ERIC ROBSON

While American historians of the nineteenth century were proclaiming the American Revolution as a triumph of liberty against tyranny, a similar interpretation was propagated in England by advocates of the Whig party there, most notably by W. E. H. Lecky and later by George Otto Trevelyan. These writers saw the Parliamentary opponents of George III as their own political ancestors, and they painted the picture of the king and his supporters in the same unflattering colors that the Americans had employed in the Declaration of Independence. In 1928 Lewis Namier challenged this interpretation of eighteenth-century politics in The Structure of Politics at the Accession of George III. *Namier showed that the political factions in Parliament under George III, whether opponents or supporters of the king, were moved less by principle than by a desire for the spoils of office. None of them was strong enough to command a majority in Parliament; none was organized as a party in the modern sense; and it was left to the king to keep the wheels of government turning.*

Neither Namier nor his disciples gave much attention in their studies to England's relations with her colonies—they were more interested in the development of British domestic politics—but Eric Robson spelled out some of the implications of Namier's view. Robson, who at the time of his death in 1954 was Lecturer in History at Manchester University, argued that the quarrel between England and the colonies, whatever its causes, could not have been the product of any thirst for unconstitutional power on the part of George III. The following passage outlines a view of George III that is widely accepted among English historians today. (Reprinted from The American Revolution in its Political and Military Aspects, *London, 1955, pp. 16-24, by permission of the estate of Eric Robson. This book in its entirety has been reprinted by the Shoe String Press, Hamden, Connecticut, 1965.)*

Why Revolution?

George III, in his own time, was accused by his opponents of attempting to subvert the system of government established by the Revolution, a charge translated by subsequent historians into one of attempting to subvert the system of responsible government.[1] The American colonists rebelled, as the argument runs, because they were the first to feel the full force of the King's assault upon liberty; their success prevented a similar effort being made in this country. Samuel Langdon, President of Harvard College, stated what became the opposition thesis as early as May 1775—that the plan of the British Government was to subjugate the colonies first, and then the whole nation, to their will. The Reverend Robert Bramley wrote to the third Duke of Portland on November 3rd, 1775, of "a regular plan of despotism" establishing among us, of which the American measures were but "one link in the chain." According to Horace Walpole, commenting on events in March 1778, the evident tendency of the King's measures was to drive all the colonies into rebellion, that all might be punished and enslaved: "I had as little doubt but if the conquest of America should be achieved, the moment of the victorious Army's return would be that of the destruction of our liberty . . . Would that Army, had it returned victorious, have hesitated to make the King as absolute as they had made him in America? Would they not have been let loose

[1] R. Sedgwick (ed.), Letters from George III to Lord Bute, 1756-1766, London, 1939, viii.

against the friends of liberty as mere rebels?" [2] In that same year, David Hartley, M.P. for Hull, a leading advocate of conciliation, saw "a design to establish an influential dominion, to be exercised at the pleasure of the Crown, and to acquire from America an independent revenue at the disposition of the Crown, uncontrolled and not accountable for to Parliament." [3] Sir George Otto Trevelyan, whose books on the American Revolution are still standard reading, fostered this argument, drawn from the contemporary opponents of George III, and carried it even further. He described the Revolution as "a defensive movement," undertaken in behalf of essential English institutions, "genuine national self-government and real ministerial responsibility against the purpose and effort of a monarch to defeat the political progress of a race." [4]

The realities of the working of the British Constitution in the eighteenth century, the absence of either genuine national self-government or real ministerial responsibility, have since been revealed by Sir Lewis Namier, Professor Richard Pares, and others; a careful reading of the manuscript sources of the reign of King George III similarly contradicts many of the absurd conclusions that have been drawn about that much maligned monarch's attitude towards the American colonies, and on the dispute between them and Great Britain. It was curious tyranny that permitted a steady growth of agitation through merchants' committees and committees of correspondence, Sons of Liberty, and similar groups, groups which did not shrink from violence whenever it seemed necessary, in large affairs like the Boston Tea Party, or in numerous smaller terrorisations and beatings of "Tories." Indeed, the attempted and unpopular reform of colonial administration in America between 1763 and 1775 was introduced with what now seems an amazing disregard of precautions, to which the key is weakness rather than tyranny. As Samuel Adams wrote in 1773, that Great Britain should continue to alienate the growing millions who

[2] J. Doran (ed.), *Journal of the Reign of King George the Third, 1771-1783,* by Horace Walpole, 2 vols., London, 1859, Vol. II, pp. 240-41.

[3] *Letters on the American War,* London, 1778, second letter. See also G. H. Guttridge, *David Hartley, M.P. An Advocate of Conciliation, 1774-1783.* Berkeley, California, 1926.

[4] G. O. Trevelyan, *The American Revolution,* 4 vols., London, 1928 edition, Vol. III, p. 161.

inhabited North America, "on whom she greatly depends, and on whose alliance in future time her existence as a nation may be suspended, is perhaps as glaring an instance of human folly as ever disgraced politicians." [5]

Those who accept the charge of tyranny levelled against George III should consider, for example, his attitude to the request of Hillsborough, Secretary of State for the American Department, for stern measures to be taken in 1769 against Massachusetts Bay and New York. Hillsborough had proposed to the Cabinet on February 13th that the appointment of the Council of Massachusetts Bay, at that time elected, should be vested in the Crown, and that the passing or entering upon the Journal of the House of Representatives of that province of any note, resolution, or order, denying or questioning the power and authority of Parliament to make laws for the province should be *ipso facto* ground for the forfeiture of the Charter. The King, in a memorandum on these proposals, wrote that the nomination of the Council by the Crown might "from a continuance of their conduct" become necessary, "but till then ought to be avoided as the altering Charters is at all times an odious measure." The second recommendation was "of so strong a nature that it rather seems calculated to increase the unhappy feudes that subsist than to asswage them." [6]

They should also ponder the position which is most clear between 1763 and 1775, that had the King wished to hold power and authority apart from the British Parliament, had he in fact held the idea of overturning the Constitution usually ascribed to him, the weapon was in his hands in the conception of a separate sovereignty in the colonies, outside Parliamentary control, which colonial leaders, who would have been his best, most obvious, and most willing allies, continued to suggest down to 1774. The opportunity existed, but was never taken. The colonial leaders believed that if the King could be made to see their argument that the colonies were governed under charters issued by him which gave them self-government, including the right of taxation (and that Parliament therefore had no power to tax them), he would be on their side.

[5] M. C. Tyler, *The Literary History of the American Revolution 1763-1783,* 2 vols. London, 1905, Vol. II, pp. 16-17.

[6] Sir J. W. Fortescue (ed.), *The Correspondence of King George III, 1760-1783,* 6 vols., London, 1927-8, Vol. II, Nos. 701 and 701A.

If anyone was making unconstitutional suggestions before 1775, it was these leaders.

In fact, the views of George III on the American colonies (and the whole Empire) remained consistent throughout the period 1760-83: a failure to move with the times, to give sufficient consideration to the existing, and rapidly developing, differences between the different components, which characterised the British approach to the problem. They were part of his conception of "our excellent and happy constitution," "the pride of all thinking minds, and the envy of all foreign nations." George III, rather than being imbued with a grossly inflated idea of the legitimate powers of the monarchy, exercised the powers which were clearly his by constitutional right and usage not in the overturning of the constitution, but in its defence. He was confronted, both at home and in the colonies, by a different conception of his position, which has triumphed since, but which was alien to both eighteenth-century theory and conditions. Throughout this period, Great Britain had not reached the stage of political development at which it would have been possible either for Parliament at home to take over the right of designating ministers and of deciding on measures, or in the colonies to remodel the Empire as a federation of self-governing states under a Crown detached from the actual government of any of its component parts.

The Crown, now the sole theoretical bond of the Empire, was in the eighteenth century still the directing factor in political life; its holder continued to do for the nation what it had not yet the means of doing adequately for itself. To contemporaries any exercise of the attributes of the Crown apart from the British Parliament would have seemed a dangerous and unconstitutional reversion to prerogative. This junction between King and Parliament in Great Britain in itself was bound to carry the supremacy of the British Parliament into the colonies; the fact that George III so thoroughly and completely stood by the constitutional principles of his time rendered a conflict between Great Britain and the colonies wellnigh inevitable. The conflict with the American colonies was engaged in and conducted by George III and his ministers to uphold the supremacy of Parliament at Westminster. It was this, rather than the rights of the Crown, which was at stake. As Lyttelton put it in 1766, in opposing the repeal of the Stamp

Act, "this is no question of expediency; it is a question of sovereignty until the Americans submit to the Legislature." The British, conceiving the Empire to be one unit—like one of Capability Brown's gardens, a tidy and symmetrical whole—were attempting to keep the colonists to their proper place in that eighteenth-century concept of Empire. It might not be the constitution as the Americans understood it, and certainly was not the constitution as they wanted it; nevertheless, it was the Constitution, pinching for the first time after 1763, because only then were the colonists brought face to face with its realities. Remoteness, and the absence of control caused by British distractions elsewhere, had mistakenly persuaded them that control by the mother-country no longer existed. Only when Parliament gave up the struggle—with General Conway's motion of February 27th, 1782, to declare impracticable the purpose of subduing the revolted colonies by force—did George III give up the "battle of the Legislature," as he had described it to Lord North on September 10th, 1775.[7] "The dreadful resolution of the 27 February last of the House of Commons," he wrote later in 1782, "this has so entirely removed the real cause of the war to the utter shame of that branch of the legislature that it would be madness not to conclude peace on the best possible terms we can obtain." [8]

This attitude of George III to the colonies is abundantly supported by evidence, hitherto mainly neglected. He stated it clearly to Dartmouth, Secretary of State for the American Department from 1772 to 1775, in that latter year. There was nothing he more earnestly desired, the King told him, than to remove the jealousies and quiet the apprehensions of his American subjects, and to see them reconciled to British government "upon principles that may secure the permanent peace and tranquility of the British Empire." He considered it his first duty in the existing situation "to maintain and support the rights of the Constitution of Great Britain." [9] Dartmouth, regarded by many as a friend to the colonists, fully accepted and appreciated this viewpoint. He himself had told General Gage, Commander-in-Chief in North America, on June

[7] Fortescue, *op. cit.*, Vol. III, No. 1709. See also Vol. IV, No. 2451.

[8] *Ibid.*, Vol. VI, No. 4004.

[9] Historical Manuscripts Commission, Fourteenth Report, Appendices, Part X. *Dartmouth Papers,* Vol. II, p. 283.

3rd, 1774, that the sovereignty of the King in Parliament over the colonies required a full and absolute submission from them. "The constitutional authority of this Kingdom over its colonies must be vindicated, and its laws obeyed throughout the whole Empire." Not only its dignity and reputation but its power and very existence were concerned: "should these ideas of independence . . . once take root, that relation between this Kingdom and its colonies, which is the bond of peace and power, will soon cease to exist and destruction must follow disunion." [10] He repeated this to Gage on March 3rd, 1775, in terms which describe not only the attitude of the King himself but also that of the majority of the politically conscious nation in this country at that time. The King considered himself "bound by every tye to exert those means the Constitution has placed in his hands for preserving that Constitution entire, and to resist with firmness every attempt to violate the rights of Parliament . . . and to encourage in the colonies ideas of independence inconsistent with their connection with this Kingdom." [11]

Herein lay the fundamental cause of the American Revolution. It was further underlined by the Solicitor-General, Alexander Wedderburn, when he replied in 1775 to Burke's plan of reconciliation, and stated the official view. The power of Parliament was defied. A portion of the King's subjects, though they had not formally cast off allegiance, were in open rebellion: such an enemy "in the bowels of the Kingdom" must be resisted, though manufactures be interrupted and commerce languish. "The integrity of the Empire is more to be regarded then the accumulation of wealth, the sufferings of individuals are nothing compared with the safety of the State." [12]

George III was fully aware of the distress and misery caused by war, and was averse to the use of force until it became the only means of restoring the American colonies to that due subordination to government which was the prerequisite of constitutional order, and which alone could preserve liberty from degenerating into licentiousness.[13] In his view, obedience to law and government

[10] C. E. Carter (ed.), *The Correspondence of General Thomas Gage,* 2 vols., New Haven, 1931-3, Vol. II, p. 165.

[11] *Ibid.,* pp. 187-9.

[12] O. S. Reid, "An Analysis of British Parliamentary Opinion on American Affairs at the close of the War of Independence," *Journal of Modern History,* XVIII, p. 221.

[13] Fortescue, *op. cit.,* Vol. I, No. 372. For the King's attitude to war, see *ibid.,* Vol. II, Nos. 841, 879, 1151, and Vol. IV, No. 2649.

was the means the Constitution had wisely framed, not only to safeguard liberty but also to have grievances removed. He had told Grafton as early as October 27th, 1768, whilst discussing dispatches from Gage openly avowing "the tendency of the town of Boston to cast off that constitutional dependency on the mother country," that such licentiousness must be curbed, yet he still insisted that policy should be motivated by "a desire with temper to let them return to their reason, not with violence to drive them." It was clear throughout to George III that if the Constitution were overthrown, "anarchy, the most terrible of all evils, must ensue," and anarchy, ever present dread of eighteenth-century statesmen, was even more dangerous in the colonies than at home, because of the risk of foreign intervention. The King's main reason for approving the changes in the Massachusetts Legislature in 1774 was precisely that it would establish "some government in that province which till now has been a scene of anarchy." By then, especially after the Boston Tea Party, an attack on property, the sacred pillar of eighteenth-century society, something more than words was required. Mediation had only served to encourage the American colonists "annually to encrease in their pretensions that thorough independency which one state has of another, but which is quite subversive of the obedience which a colony owes to its mother country." [14] The present relations between this country and the Dominions have done nothing to lessen uninformed criticism of British policy before 1775, when such relations were hardly dreamt of, and are a further striking example of the care which is necessary (but hardly ever applied) not to read past happenings in the light of present conceptions, particularly those of the reign of George III in both political and imperial affairs.

[14] *Ibid.*, Vol. III, No. 1379, George III to Lord North, February 4th, 1774.

8.

LAWRENCE HENRY GIPSON

With the rise of history as an academic profession in the twentieth century there began a new examination not merely of the American Revolution but of the whole history of the American colonies under British rule. The new historians, among whom the pioneers were Herbert Levi Osgood, George Louis Beer, and Charles McLean Andrews, tried to see the colonies primarily as a part of the empire, viewing them from the perspective of London rather than Philadelphia or Boston. The result was a sympathetic understanding of imperial policies that American historians had previously judged only with reference to their impact in the colonies. In the new perspective the old British Empire could be seen to have possessed far more virtues than historians had suspected. The culminating product of this new, broader approach to early American history, so far as the Revolutionary period is concerned, is the monumental series by Lawrence Henry Gipson, The British Empire before the American Revolution, *the last volumes of which will present a full-scale account of the Revolution seen in the context of the whole empire. Professor Gipson's interpretation was adumbrated in the following essay, originally published in 1950 and revised by the author for publication here. Professor Gipson has stated that he regards the essay as, in a sense, the crux of his whole series. (Reprinted from* Political Science Quarterly, *Vol. LXV, March 1950, pp. 86-104, by permission of the author and publisher, and with revisions by the author.)*

The American Revolution as an Aftermath of the Great War for the Empire, 1754-1763

Great wars in modern times have too frequently been the breeders of revolution. The exhausting armed struggles in which France became engaged in the latter half of the eighteenth century led as directly to the French Revolution as did the First World War to the Russian Revolution; it may be said as truly that the American Revolution was an aftermath of the Anglo-French conflict in the New World carried on between 1754 and 1763. This is by no means to deny that other factors were involved in the launching of these revolutionary movements. Before proceeding with an analysis of the theme of this paper, however, it would be well to consider the wording of the title given to it.[1]

Words may be used either to disguise or to distort facts as well as to clarify them, but the chief task of the historian is to illuminate the past. He is faced, therefore, with the responsibility of using only such words as will achieve this broad objective of his calling and to reject those that obscure or defeat it. For this reason "the French and Indian War," as a term descriptive of the conflict to which we have just referred, has been avoided in this essay as well as in the writer's series on the *British Empire before the American Revolution.* This has been done in spite of the fact that it has been employed by most Americans ever since the early days of our Republic and therefore has the sanction of long usage as well as the sanction of American national tradition which assigns to the Revolutionary War a position of such commanding importance as to make all other events in American history, preceding as well as following it, quite subordinate to it. In contrast to this traditional interpretation of our history one may affirm that the Anglo-French conflict settled nothing less than the incomparably vital question as to what civil-

[1] This paper was read before the colonial history section of the American Historical Association in December 1948 at the Annual Meeting held in Washington.

ization—what complex cultural patterns, what political institutions—would arise in the great Mississippi basin and the valleys of the rivers draining it, a civilization, whatever it might be, surely destined to expand to the Pacific seaboard and finally to dominate the North American continent. The determination of this crucial issue is perhaps the most momentous event in the life of the English-speaking people in the New World and quite overshadows in importance both the Revolutionary War and the later Civil War, events which, it is quite clear, were each contingent upon the outcome of the earlier crisis.

A struggle of such proportions, involving tremendous stakes, deserves a name accurately descriptive of its place in the history of the English-speaking people, and the title "the French and Indian War," as suggested, in no way fulfills this need. For the war was not, as the name would seem to imply, a conflict largely between English and French New World colonials and their Indian allies, nor was it localized in North America to the extent that the name would appear to indicate. In contrast, it was waged both before and after an open declaration of war by the British and French nations with all their resources for nine years on three oceans, and much of the land washed by the waters of them, and it ultimately brought in both Spain, allied to France, and Portugal, allied to Great Britain. While it is true, as the name would connote, that it involved wilderness fighting, yet of equal, if not greater importance in assessing its final outcome was the pouring forth of Britain's financial resources in a vast program of shipbuilding, in the equipment and support of the British and colonial armies and the royal navy, and in the subsidization both of allies on the European continent and of the colonies in America. If it also involved the reduction of the fortress of Louisbourg, Fort Niagara, Fort Duquesne, Quebec and Montreal in North America, each in turn to fall to British regulars aided by American provincial troops, these successes, of great significance, were, in fact, really contingent upon the resounding British naval victories in the Mediterranean, off the Strait of Gibraltar, in the Bay of Biscay, and elsewhere, that brought about the virtual extinction of the French navy and merchant marine and thereby presented to France—seeking to supply her forces in Canada and elsewhere with adequate reinforcements and materiel—a logistical problem so insoluble as to spell the doom of her North American empire and of her possessions in India and elsewhere.

If the term "the French and Indian War" meets none of the requirements of accurate historical nomenclature, neither does the term "the Seven Years' War"—a name appropriately enough employed by historians to designate the mighty conflict that raged for seven years in Germany before its conclusion in the Treaty of Hubertusburg in 1763. The principals in this war were Prussia, allied with Great Britain, Hanover, Brunswick and Hesse, facing Austria, most of the Holy Roman Empire, Russia and Sweden, all allied with France and receiving subsidies from her. Although George II, as King of Great Britain and Elector of Hanover, in the treaty of 1758 with Frederick of Prussia, promised not to conclude peace without mutual agreement with the latter, and although large subsidies were annually paid to Prussia as well as to the other continental allies out of the British treasury and troops were also sent to Germany, it must be emphasized that these aids were designed primarily for the protection of the King's German Electorate. In other words, the British alliance in no way supported the objectives of the Prussian King, when he suddenly began the German war in 1756 by invading Saxony—two years after the beginning of the Anglo-French war. In this connection it should be borne in mind that throughout the Seven Years' War in Germany Great Britain remained at peace with both Russia and Sweden and refused therefore to send a fleet into the Baltic in spite of the demands of Frederick that this be done; nor were British land troops permitted to assist him against Austria, but only to help form a protective shield for Hanover against the thrusts of the French armies. For the latter were determined not only to overrun the Electorate—something that they succeeded in doing—but to hold it as a bargaining point to be used at the conclusion of hostilities with Great Britain, a feat, however, beyond their power of accomplishment. Closely related and intertwined as were the two wars, they were, nevertheless, distinct in their beginning and distinct in their termination.

Indeed, while British historians at length were led to adopt the nomenclature applied by German and other continental historians to all hostilities that took place between 1754 and 1763 in both the

Old and New Worlds, American historians, by and large in the past, have rejected, and rightly so, it seems, the name "the Seven Years' War" to designate specifically the struggle during these years in North America with the fate of that continent at stake; so likewise many of them have rejected, as equally inadmissible, the name "the French and Indian War." Instead, the late Professor Osgood employed the title "the Fourth Intercolonial War," surely not a good one; George Bancroft called the war "the American Revolution: First Phase," still more inaccurate in some respects than the names he sought to avoid; Francis Parkman, with the flare of a romanticist, was at first inclined to call it "the Old French War" but finally, under the influence of the great-man-in-history thesis, gave to his two remarkable volumes concerned with it the totally misleading name, *Montcalm and Wolfe;* finally, John Fiske, the philosopher-historian, as luminous in his views as he was apt to be careless in the details of historical scholarship, happily fastened upon the name "the Great War." In the series on the *British Empire before the American Revolution* the writer has built upon Fiske's title and has called it "the Great War for the Empire." He has done so in order to emphasize not only the fact that the war was a very great conflict both in its scope and in its lasting effects—as Fiske saw it with clearness—but also that it was a war entered into specifically for the defense of the British Empire and was by far the most important ever waged by Great Britain to this end.

It may be pointed out that later charges, especially by American writers, that the war was begun by Great Britain with less worthy motives in mind, are not supported by the great mass of state papers and the private correspondence of British statesmen responsible for making the weighty decisions at the time—materials now available to the student which the writer has attempted to analyze in detail in the two volumes of his series that appeared under the title of *Zones of International Friction, 1748-1754.* In other words, the idea that the war was started as the result of European balance-of-power politics or by British mercantilists for the purpose of destroying a commercial rival and for conquering Canada and the French West Indies, and for expelling the French from India, rather than for the much more limited and legitimate objective of affording the colonies (particularly the new province of Nova Scotia and the Old Dominion of Virginia) protection against the aggressive aims of France, must be dismissed by students brought face to face with impressive evidence to the contrary.

The development of the war into one for the military mastery of the North American continent came with the growing conviction on the part of the British ministers that nothing short of this drastic step would realize the primary aims of the government in arriving at the determination, as the result of appeals from the colonies for assistance, to challenge the right of French troops to be planted well within the borders of the Nova Scotia peninsula and at the forks of the Ohio. One may go as far as to state that the acquisition of Canada—as an objective sought by mercantilists to contribute to the wealth of Great Britain—would have seemed fantastic to any contemporary who had the slightest knowledge of the tremendous financial drain that that great possession had been on the treasury of the French king for over a century before 1754. Moreover, the motives that ultimately led, after much searching of heart, to its retention after its conquest by Great Britain were not commercial but strategic and had primarily in view the security and welfare generally of the older American colonies.

In view of these facts, not to be confused with surmises, the name "the Great War for the Empire" seems to the writer not only appropriate but among all the names heretofore applied to the war in question by far the most suitable that can be used by anyone concerned with the history of the old British Empire who seeks earnestly to maintain that standard of exactness in terminology, as well as in other respects, which the public has a right to demand of him.

The description just given of the motives that led to the Great War for the Empire, nevertheless, runs counter, as suggested, to American national tradition and most history that has been written by American historians in harmony with it. This tradition had a curious beginning. It arose partly out of Pitt's zealous efforts to energize the colonies to prosecute the war most actively; but there also was another potent factor involved in its creation. Before the conclusion of hostilities in 1763 certain powerful commercial interests—centered particularly at Newport, Rhode Island, Boston, New York City, and to a less extent in Philadelphia—in a desire to continue an enormously lucrative trade with the French West

Indies, and therefore with the enemy, all in the face of Pitt's determination to keep supplies from the French armed forces operating in the New World, began to express themselves in terms that implied that the war was peculiarly Great Britain's war and only incidentally one that concerned her colonies and that the French, really friendly to the aspirations of British colonials, were opposed only to the mercantilistic ambitions of the mother country. By 1766 —just twelve years after the beginning of the war and three years after its termination—this extraordinary tradition had become so well established that Benjamin Franklin, astonishingly enough, could actually assert in his examination before a committee of the House of Commons:

> I know the last war is commonly spoke of here as entered into for the defence, or for the sake of the people of America; I think it is quite misunderstood. It began about the limits between Canada and Nova Scotia, about territories to which the crown indeed laid claim, but were not claimed by any British colony. . . . We had therefore no particular concern or interest in that dispute. As to the Ohio, the contest there began about your right of trading in the Indian country, a right you had by the Treaty of Utrecht, which the French infringed . . . they took a fort which a company of your merchants, and their factors and correspondents, had erected there to secure that trade. Braddock was sent with an army to retake that fort . . . and to protect your trade. It was not until after his defeat that the colonies were attacked. They were before in perfect peace with both French and Indians. . . .

By the beginning of 1768 the tradition had been so extended that John Dickinson—voicing the popular American view in his highly important *Letters from a Farmer in Pennsylvania,* No. VIII—felt that he not only could affirm, as did Franklin, that the war was strictly Britain's war and fought for selfish purposes, but could even insist that the acquisition of territory in North America as the result of it "is greatly injurious to these colonies" and that they therefore were not under the slightest obligation to the mother country.

But to return to the last phases of the Great War for the Empire. The British customs officials—spurred into unusual activity in the face of Pitt's demand for the strict enforcement of the Trade and Navigation Acts in order to break up the pernicious practice of bringing aid and comfort to the enemy—were led to employ writs of assistance for the purpose of laying their hands upon goods landed in American ports and secured in exchange for American provisions sent for the most part either directly or indirectly to the French West Indies. Although in the midst of hostilities, most of the merchants in Boston showed bitter opposition to the writs and equally ardent support of James Otis' declaration made in open court in 1761 that Parliament, acting within the limits of the constitution, was powerless to extend the use of these writs to America, whatever its authority might be in Great Britain. The importance of this declaration lies not so much in its immediate effect but rather in the fact that it was indicative of the line of attack that would subsequently be followed not only by Otis but also the Adamses, Hawley, Hancock, and other popular leaders in the Bay colony during the developing crisis as they sought on constitutional grounds to challenge the power of Parliament to legislate for America. Further, it is clear that, even before the Great War for the Empire had been terminated, there were those in the province who had begun to view Great Britain as the real enemy rather than France.

Just as definitely related to the war under consideration as the issue over writs of assistance was that growing out of the twopenny acts of the Virginia Assembly. In search of funds for maintaining the frontier defensive forces under the command of Colonel George Washington, the Assembly was led to pass in 1755 and 1758 those highly questionable laws as favorable to the tobacco planters as they were indefensively unjust to the clergy. Even assuming the fact that these laws were war measures, and therefore in a sense emergency measures, it was inconceivable that the Privy Council would permit so palpable a violation of contractual relations as they involved. The royal disallowance of the laws in question opened the way for Patrick Henry, the year that hostilities were terminated by the Peace of Paris, not only to challenge in the Louisa County courthouse the right of the King in Council to refuse to approve any law that a colony might pass that in its judgment was a good law, but to affirm that such refusal was nothing less than an act of tyranny on the part of the King. It was thus resentment at the overturning of Virginia war legislation that led to this attack upon the judicial authority of review by the Crown—an authority exercised previously without serious protest for over a century. It should also be noted that the Henry thesis helped to lay the foundation for the theory of the equality of colonial laws with those passed by Parliament, a theory of the constitution of the empire that most American leaders in 1774 had come to accept in arguing that if the King could no longer exercise a veto over the acts of the legislature of Great Britain, it was unjust that he should do so over those of the colonial assemblies.

But the most fateful aftermath of the Great War for the Empire, with respect to the maintenance of the historic connection between the mother country and the colonies, grew out of the problem of the control and support not only of the vast trans-Appalachian interior—the right to which was now confirmed by treaty to Great Britain—but of the new acquisitions in North America secured from France and Spain. Under the terms of the royal Proclamation of 1763, French Canada to the east of the Great Lakes was organized as the Province of Quebec; most of old Spanish Florida became the Province of East Florida; and those areas, previously held by Spain as well as by France to the west of the Apalachicola and to the east of New Orleans and its immediate environs, became the Province of West Florida. The Proclamation indicated that proper inducements would be offered British and other Protestants to establish themselves in these new provinces. With respect to the trans-Appalachian region, however, it created there a temporary but vast Indian reserve by laying down as a barrier the crest of the mountains beyond which there should be no white settlement except by specific permission of the Crown.

The Proclamation has been represented not only as a blunder, the result largely of carelessness and ignorance on the part of those responsible for it, but also as a cynical attempt by the British ministry to embody mercantilistic principles in an American land policy that in itself ran counter to the charter limits of many of the colonies and the interests in general of the colonials. Nevertheless, this view of the Proclamation fails to take into account the fact that it was the offspring of the war and that the trans-Appalachian aspects of it were an almost inevitable result of promises made during the progress of hostilities. For both in the Treaty of Easton in 1758 with the Ohio Valley Indians, a treaty ratified by the Crown, and in the asseverations of such military leaders as Colonel Bouquet, these Indians were assured that they would be secure in their trans-Appalachian lands as a reward for deserting their allies, the French. As a sign of good faith, the lands lying within the bounds of Pennsylvania to the west of the mountains, purchased by the Proprietors from the Six Nations in 1754, were solemnly released. Thus committed in honor in the course of the war, what could the Cabinet Council at its termination do other than it finally did in issuing the Proclamation of 1763? But this step was in opposition to the interests of such groups of land speculators as, for example, the Patrick Henry group in Virginia and the Richard Henderson group in North Carolina, both of whom boldly ignored the Proclamation in negotiating with the Cherokee Indians for land grants. It also led to open defiance of this imperial regulation by frontiersmen who, moving beyond the mountains by the thousands, proceeded to settle within the Indian reserve—some on lands previously occupied before the beginning of the late war or before the great Indian revolt in 1763, and others on new lands.

The Proclamation line of 1763 might have become an issue, indeed a most formidable one, between the government of Great Britain and the colonials, had not the former acquiesced in the inevitable and confirmed certain Indian treaties that provided for the transfer of much of the land which had been the particular object of quest on the part of speculators and of those moving westward from the settled areas to establish new homes. Such were the treaties of Hard Labor, Fort Stanwix, Lochaber, and the modification of the last-named by the Donelson agreement with the Cherokees in 1771. Nor did the regulation of the trans-Appalachian Indian trade create serious colonial irritation, especially in view of the failure of the government to implement the elaborate Board of Trade plan drawn up in 1764. The same, however, cannot be said of the program put forward by the ministry and accepted by Parliament for securing the means to maintain order and provide protection for this vast area and the new acquisitions to the north and south of it.

Theoretically, it would have been possible for the government of Great Britain to have dropped onto the lap of the old continental colonies the entire responsibility for maintaining garrisons at various strategic points in North America—in Canada, about the Great

Lakes, in the Ohio and Mississippi valleys, and in East and West Florida. In spite, however, of assertions made by some prominent colonials, such as Franklin, in 1765 and 1766 that the colonies would be able and were willing to take up the burden of providing for the defense of America, this, under the circumstances, was utterly chimerical. For it would have involved not only a vast expenditure of funds but also highly complicated inter-colonial arrangements, even in the face of the most serious inter-colonial rivalry (for example, that between Pennsylvania and Virginia respecting the control of the upper Ohio Valley). The very proportions of the task made it an insuperable obstacle to leave to the colonies; the colonies, moreover, would have been faced by another impediment almost as difficult to surmount—the utter aversion of Americans of the eighteenth century, by and large, to the dull routine of garrison duty. This was emphasized by the Massachusetts Bay Assembly in 1755 in its appeal to the government of Great Britain, after Braddock's defeat, to send regulars to man the frontier forts of that province; the dispatches of Colonel George Washington in 1756 and in 1757 respecting the shameful desertion of militiamen, ordered to hold the chain of posts on the western frontier of Virginia in order to check the frightful French and Indian raids, support this position, as does the testimony in 1757 of Governor Lyttelton of South Carolina, who made clear that the inhabitants of that colony were not at all adapted to this type of work. The post-war task of garrison duty was clearly one to be assumed by regulars held to their duty under firm discipline and capable of being shifted from one strategic point to another as circumstances might require. Further, to be effective, any plan for the defense of the new possessions and the trans-Appalachian region demanded unity of command, something the colonies could not provide. Manifestly this could be done only through the instrumentalities of the mother country.

The British ministry, thus confronted with the problem of guaranteeing the necessary security for the extended empire in North America—which it was estimated would involve the annual expenditure of from three to four hundred thousand pounds for the maintenance of ten thousand troops (according to various estimates made by General Amherst and others in 1764 and to be found among the Shelburne Papers)—was impelled to raise the question: Should not the colonials be expected to assume some definite part of the cost of this? In view of the feeling that they were in a position to do so and that the stability of these outlying possessions was a matter of greater concern and importance generally to them, by reason of their proximity, than to the people of the mother country three thousand miles away, the ministry's answer was in the affirmative. The reason for this is not hard to fathom. The nine years of war had involved Britons in tremendous expenditures. In spite of very heavy taxation during these years, the people were left saddled at the termination of hostilities with a national debt, of unprecedented proportions for that day and age, of over one hundred and forty million pounds. It was necessary not only to service and to retire this debt, in so far as was possible, but also to meet the ordinary demands of the civil government and to maintain the navy at a point of strength that would offer some assurance that France and Spain would have no desire in the future to plan a war to recover their territorial losses. In addition to all this, there was now the problem of meeting the charges necessary for keeping the new possessions in North America under firm military control both for their internal good order and for protection from outside interference.

It may be noted that before the war the British budget had called for average annual expenditures of six and a half million pounds; between the years 1756 and 1766 these expenditures mounted to fourteen and a half million pounds a year on the average and from the latter date to 1775 ranged close to ten million pounds. As a result, the annual per capita tax in Great Britain, from 1763 to 1775, without considering local rates, was many times the average annual per capita tax in even those American colonies that made the greatest contribution to the Great War for the Empire, such as Massachusetts Bay and Connecticut—without reference to those colonies that had done little or nothing in this conflict, and therefore had accumulated little in the way of a war debt, such as Maryland and Georgia. The student of the history of the old British Empire, in fact, should accept with great reserve statements to the contrary—some of them quite irresponsible in nature—made by Americans during the heat of the controversy, with respect to the nature of the public burdens they were obliged to carry in the years preceding the outbreak of the Revolutionary War. In this connection a study of parliamentary reimbursement of colonial war expenses from 1756 to 1763 in its relation to public debts in America between the years 1763 and 1775 is most revealing.[1] As to American public finance, all that space will here permit is to state that there is abundant evidence to indicate that, during the five-year period preceding the outbreak of the Revolutionary War, had the inhabitants of any of the thirteen colonies (including those of Massachusetts Bay and Virginia) been taxed in one of those years at the average high per capita rate that the British people were taxed from 1760 to 1775, the proceeds of that one year's tax would have taken care of the ordinary expenditures of the colony in question for that year and quite liquidated its war debt, so little of which remained in any of the colonies by 1770.[2] Well may John Adams have admitted in 1780 what was equally true in 1770: "America is not used to great taxes, and the people there are not yet disciplined to such enormous taxation as in England."

Assuming, as did the Grenville ministry in 1764, the justice of expecting the Americans to share in the cost of policing the new possessions in North America, the simplest and most obvious way, it might appear, to secure this contribution to a common end so important to both Americans and Britons was to request the colonial governments to make definite grants of funds. This was the requisition or quota system that had been employed in the course of the recent war. But the most obvious objections to it were voiced that same year by Benjamin Franklin who, incidentally, was to reverse himself the following year in conferring with Grenville as the Pennsylvania London agent. In expressing confidentially his personal, rather than any official, views to his friend Richard Jackson on June 25, 1764 he declared: "Quota's [sic] would be difficult to settle at first with Equality, and would, if they could be made equal at first, soon become unequal, and never would be satisfactory." Indeed, practical experience with this system as a settled method of guaranteeing even the minimum essential resources for the end in view, had shown its weakness and utter unfairness. If it could not work equitably even in war time, could it be expected to work in time of peace? It is thus not surprising that this method of securing

[1] See in my series, *The British Empire before the American Revolution*, Volume X, chap. 2.

[2] See *Ibid.*, chaps. 3-5.

even a portion of the funds required for North American security should have been rejected in favor of some plan that presented better prospects of a definite American revenue.

The plan of last resort to the ministry was therefore to ask Parliament to act. That Grenville, however, was aware that serious objections might be raised against any direct taxation of the colonials by the government of Great Britain is indicated by the caution with which he approached the solution of the problem of securing from America about a third of the total cost of its defense. First of all the so-called Sugar Act was passed at his request. This provided for import duties on certain West Indian and other products. Colonial import duties imposed by Parliament, at least since 1733, were no innovation. But the anticipated yield of these duties fell far short of the desired one hundred thousand pounds. In introducing the bill for the above Act, he therefore raised the question of a stamp duty but requested postponement of parliamentary action until the colonial governments had been consulted. The latter were thereupon requested to make any suggestions for ways of raising an American fund that might seem more proper to the people than such a tax. Further, it would appear—at least, according to various London advices published in Franklin and Hall's *Pennsylvania Gazette*—that during the fall of 1764 proposals were seriously considered by the Cabinet Council for extending representation in Parliament to the colonies through the election of members to the House of Commons by various colonial assemblies. However, it is quite clear that by the beginning of 1765 any proposals of this nature that might have been under deliberation by the ministry, had been put aside when Grenville at length had become convinced that representation in Parliament was neither actively sought nor even desired by Americans. For the South Carolina Commons House of Assembly went strongly on record against this idea in September 1764 as did the Virginia House of Burgesses in December. In fact, when in the presence of the London colonial agents the minister had outlined the objections raised by Americans to the idea of such representation, not one of them, including Franklin, was prepared to deny the validity of these objections. That he was not mistaken about the opposition of Americans at large to sending members to Parliament, in spite of the advocacy of this by James Otis, is made clear in the resolutions passed by other colonial assemblies in addition to South Carolina and Virginia and by the Stamp Act Congress in 1765. Indeed, in 1768 the House of Representatives of Massachusetts Bay, in its famous Circular Letter framed in opposition to the Townshend duties, went so far as to make clear that the people of that colony actually preferred taxation by Parliament without representation to such taxation with representation.

When—in view of the failure of the colonial governments to suggest any practicable, alternate plan for making some contribution to the post-war defensive program in North America—Grenville finally urged in Parliament the passage of an American stamp bill, he acted on an unwarranted assumption. This assumption was—paraphrasing the minister's remarks to the colonial agents in 1765—that opposition to stamp taxes for the specific purpose in mind would disappear in America both in light of the benefits such provision would bring to colonials in general and by reason of the plain justice of the measure itself; further that, in place of opposition, an atmosphere of mutual goodwill would be generated by a growing recognition on the part of Americans that they could trust the benevolence of the mother country to act with fairness to all within the empire. Instead, with the news of the passage of the act, cries of British tyranny and impending American slavery soon resounded throughout the entire eastern Atlantic seaboard. What would have been the fate of the empire had Grenville remained in office to attempt to enforce the act, no one can say. But as members of the opposition to the Rockingham ministry, he and his brother, Earl Temple, raised their voices—one as a commoner, the other as a peer—in warning that the American colonies would inevitably be lost to the empire should Parliament be led to repeal the act in the face of colonial resistance and the pressure of British merchants. Had Parliament determined, in spite of violence and threats of violence, to enforce the act, this might have meant open rebellion and civil war ten years before it actually occurred. Instead, this body decided to yield and, in spite of the passing of the so-called Declaratory Act setting forth its fundamental powers to legislate on all matters relating to the empire, suffered a loss of prestige in the New World that was never to be regained.

But the Stamp Act was not the sole object of attack by colonials. To many of them not only the Sugar Act of 1764 but the whole English pre-war trade and navigation system was equally, if not actually more, obnoxious. Indeed, the unusual energy displayed by the navy and the customs officials—spurred into action by Pitt during the latter years of the war—brought about the condemnation in courts of vice-admiralty of many American vessels whose owners were guilty of serious trade violations or greater crimes and generated a degree of antagonism against the whole body of late seventeenth- and early eighteenth-century restrictions on commercial intercourse such as had never previously existed. It is not without significance that the greatest acts of terrorism and destruction during the great riot of August 1765 in Boston were directed not against the Massachusetts Bay stamp distributor but against those officials responsible for encouraging and supporting the enforcement, during the late war, of the various trade acts passed long before its beginning in 1754. The hatred also of the Rhode Island merchants, as a group, against the restrictions of the navigation system as well as against the Sugar Act of 1764, remained constant. Moreover, in December 1766 most of the New York merchants, over two hundred in number, showed their repugnance to the way that this system was functioning by sending a strongly worded petition to the House of Commons in which they enumerated an impressive list of grievances that they asked to be redressed. Even Chatham, the great friend of America, called their petition "highly improper: in point of time most absurd, in the extent of their pretensions, most excessive; and in the reasoning, most grossly fallacious and offensive." In fact, all the leading men in Great Britain supported the system of trade restrictions.

In view especially of the great financial burden that the late war had placed upon the mother country, the government now determined to enforce the trade and navigation laws in a more effective way than had been done before 1754. To that end it passed in 1767 appropriate legislation levying import duties that would provide funds from the colonies by means of which public officials in America could be held to greater accountability, since their salaries could be paid directly by the Crown. Such legislation could have only one result: the combined resistance of those, on the one hand, opposed to any type of taxation that Parliament might apply to America and of those, on the other, desiring to free the colonies of hampering trade restrictions.

The suggestion on the part of the Continental Congress in 1774 that Americans would uphold the British navigation system, if exempted from parliamentary taxation, while a shrewd gesture to win support in England, would seem to have had no other real significance. For it is utterly inconceivable that the Congress itself, or the individual colonial governments, could have set up machinery capable of preventing violations of the system at will on the part of those whose financial interests were adversely affected by its operation. Moreover, it is obvious that, by the time the news had reached America that Lord North's ministry had secured the passage of the coercive acts—for the most part directed against Massachusetts Bay for the defiant destruction of the East India Company's tea—leading colonials, among them Franklin, had arrived at the conclusion that Parliament possessed powers so very limited with respect to the empire that without the consent of the local assemblies it could pass neither constitutional nor fiscal legislation that affected Americans and the framework of their governments. It is equally obvious that this represented a most revolutionary position when contrasted with that held by Franklin and the other delegates to the Albany Congress twenty years earlier. For it was there in 1754 that the famous Plan of Union was drawn up and approved by the Congress—a plan based upon the assumption by the framers of the Plan that Parliament, not the Crown, had supreme authority within the empire, and that this authority alone was adequate to bring about fundamental changes in the constitutions of the colonies in order legally to clothe the proposed union government with adequate fiscal and other powers.

In accounting for the radical change in attitude of many leading colonials between the years 1754 and 1774 respecting the nature of the constitution of the empire, surely among the factors that must be weighed is the truly overwhelming victory achieved in the Great War for the Empire. This victory not only freed colonials for the first time in the history of the English-speaking people in the New World from dread of the French, their Indian allies, and the Spaniards, but, what is of equal significance, opened up to them the prospect, if given freedom of action, of a vast growth of power and wealth in the course of an inevitable westward expansion. Indeed, it is abundantly clear that, in the eyes of many Americans by 1774, a continued subordination of the colonies to the government of Great Britain was no longer considered the asset it had been judged by them to be in 1754, but rather an onerous liability. What, for instance, had the debt-ridden mother country to offer in 1774 to the now geographically secure, politically mature, prosperous, dynamic, and self-reliant offspring along the Atlantic seaboard, except the dubious opportunity of accepting new, as well as retaining old, burdens? And these burdens would have to be borne in order to lighten somewhat the great financial load that the taxpayers of Great Britain were forced to carry by reason of obligations the nation had assumed both in the course of the late war and at its termination. If many Americans thought they had a perfect right to profit personally by trading with the enemy in time of war, how much more deeply must they have resented in time of peace the serious efforts made by the home government to enforce the elaborate restrictions on commercial intercourse? Again, if, even after the defeat of Colonel Washington at Great Meadows in 1754, colonials such as Franklin were opposed to paying any tax levied by Parliament for establishing a fund for the defense of North America, how much more must they have been inclined to oppose such taxation to that end with the passing in 1763 of the great international crisis?

At this point the question must be frankly faced: If France had won the war decisively and thereby consolidated her position and perfected her claims in Nova Scotia, as well as to the southward of the St. Lawrence, in the Great Lakes region, and in the Ohio and Mississippi valleys, is it at all likely that colonials would have made so fundamental a constitutional issue of the extension to them of the principle of the British stamp tax? Would they have resisted such a tax had Parliament imposed it in order to provide on an equitable basis the maximum resources for guaranteeing their safety, at a time when they were faced on their highly restricted borders by a militant, victorious enemy having at its command thousands of ferocious redskins? Again, accepting the fact of Britain's victory, is it not reasonable to believe that, had Great Britain at the close of the triumphant war left Canada to France and carefully limited her territorial demands in North America to those comparatively modest objectives that she had in mind at its beginning, there would have been no very powerful movement within the foreseeable future toward complete colonial autonomy—not to mention American independence? Would not Americans have continued to feel the need as in the past to rely for their safety and welfare upon British sea power and British land power, as well as upon British resources generally? In other words, was Governor Thomas Hutchinson of Massachusetts Bay far mistaken when, in analyzing the American situation late in 1773, he affirmed in writing to the Earl of Dartmouth:

> Before the peace [of 1763] I thought nothing so much to be desired as the cession of Canada. I am now convinced that if it had remained to the French none of the spirit of opposition to the Mother Country would have yet appeared & I think the effects of it [that is, the cession of Canada] worse than all we had to fear from the French or Indians.

In conclusion, it may be said that most colonials in the eighteenth century at one time or another felt strongly the desire for a wider expression of freedom of action than was legally permitted before 1754. Indeed, one can readily uncover these strong impulses even in the early part of the seventeenth century. Yet Americans were, by and large, realists, as were the British, and under the functioning of the imperial system from, let us say, 1650 to 1750 great mutual advantages were enjoyed, with a fair division, taking everything into consideration, of the financial burdens necessary to support the system. However, the mounting Anglo-French rivalry in North America from 1750 onward, the outbreak of hostilities in 1754, and the subsequent nine years of fighting destroyed the old equilibrium, leaving the colonials after 1760 in a highly favored position compared to the taxpayers of Great Britain. Attempts on the part of the Crown and Parliament to restore by statute the old balance led directly to the American constitutional crisis, out of which came the Revolutionary War and the establishment of American independence. Such, ironically, was the aftermath of the Great War for the Empire, a war that Britons believed, as the Earl of Shelburne affirmed in 1762 in Parliament, was begun for the "security of the British colonies in N. America. . . ."

9.

THE AMERICAN REVOLUTION: REVISIONS IN NEED OF REVISING

The period since the close of the Second World War has seen the beginning of a reaction not only from the interpretation of the Revolution as a social movement but also from the imperial, the Namierist, and the economic interpretation. The following essay, delivered as an address, by the editor of this volume, at the meeting of the Mississippi Valley Historical Association in 1956, suggests some of the reasons for such a reaction. (Reprinted from William and Mary Quarterly, *third series, Vol. XIV, January 1957, pp. 3-15).*

The American Revolution: Revisions in Need of Revising

During the past fifty years three ideas have inspired research into the history of the eighteenth century in America and England. The earliest of these to appear, and the most fruitful of results, was the idea that American colonial history must be seen in the setting of the British Empire as a whole. We are all familiar today with the new insights and new discoveries that have grown out of this view: the great works of George Louis Beer and Charles McLean Andrews, the monumental synthesis of Professor Lawrence Gipson, which now approaches its culmination. This has been a great idea, and it has done more than any other to shape our understanding of the colonial past.

A second idea, which has affected in one way or another most of us who study colonial history, is that the social and economic divisions of a people will profoundly influence the course of their history. This idea received early application to American history in Carl Becker's study of New York politics on the eve of the Revolution and in Charles Beard's *An Economic Interpretation of the Constitution*. New York politics before the Revolution, Becker said, revolved around two questions, equally important, the question of home rule and that of who should rule at home.[1] Subsequent historians have found in Becker's aphorism a good description of the Revolutionary period as a whole. The conflict between different social groups now looms as large in our histories of the Revolution as the struggle against England. Like all seminal ideas, this one has sometimes been used as a substitute for research instead of a stimulus to it. Historians have been so convinced of the importance of social and economic divisions that they have uttered the wildest kind of nonsense, for example, about the social and economic basis of a religious movement like the Great Awakening of the 1740's. The view has nevertheless been productive of important new insights and new information.

The third idea, although it has had scarcely any effect as yet on the study of American history, has furnished the principal impetus to recent research in British history. It is a more complex idea, growing out of the discoveries of Sir Lewis Namier. The effect of these discoveries has been to attach a new importance to local as opposed to national forces. "It has been the greatest of Sir Lewis Namier's achievements," says Richard Pares, "to exhibit the personal and local nature of political issues and political power at this time." [2] Namier and his disciples, of whom Pares is the most notable, have destroyed the traditional picture of British politics in the age of the American Revolution. During this period, they tell us, there were no political parties in the modern sense, nor were there any political factions or associations with any principle or belief beyond that of serving selfish or local interests. The Rockingham Whigs,

[1] Carl Becker, *The History of Political Parties in the Province of New York, 1760-1776* (Madison, Wis., 1909), p. 22.
[2] Richard Pares, *King George III and the Politicians* (Oxford, 1953), p. 2.

who made such a display of their opposition to the repressive measures against the colonies, were no different from the other squabbling factions except in their hypocritical pretense of standing for broader principles. And George III owed his control over Parliament not to bribery and corruption but simply to his constitutional position in the government and to his skill as a politician during a time when the House of Commons lacked effective leaders of its own.

Each of these three ideas, the imperial, the social or economic, and the Namierist, has had a somewhat similar effect on our understanding of the American Revolution. That effect has been to discredit, in different ways, the old Whig interpretation. The imperial historians have examined the running of the empire before the Revolution and pronounced it fair. The Navigation Acts, they have shown, were no cause for complaint. The Board of Trade did as good a job as could be expected. The Admiralty Courts were a useful means of maintaining fair play and fair trade on the high seas. Indeed, Professor Gipson tells us, the old colonial system "may not unfairly be compared to modern systems of state interference with the liberty of the subject in matters involving industry and trade, accepting the differences involved in the nature of the regulations respectively. In each case, individuals or groups within the state are forbidden to follow out lines of action that, while highly beneficial to those locally or personally concerned, are considered inimical to the larger national objectives." [3] In the light of such imperial benevolence and farsightedness, the unwillingness of the Americans to pay the trifling contribution demanded of them in the sixties and seventies becomes small and mean, and the resounding rhetoric of a Henry or an Otis or an Adams turns into the bombast of a demagogue.

The social and economic interpretation does nothing to redeem the fallen Revolutionary patriots but rather shows them up as hypocrites pursuing selfish interests while they mouth platitudes about democracy and freedom. Their objections to parliamentary taxation are reduced to mere tax evasion, with the arguments shifting as the character of the taxes shifted. Their insistence on freedom and equality is shown to be insincere, because in setting up their

[3] Lawrence H. Gipson, *The British Empire before the American Revolution*, III (Caldwell, Idaho, 1936), 287.

own governments they failed to establish universal suffrage or proportional representation. They were, it would appear, eager to keep one foot on the lower classes while they kicked the British with the other.

Namier and his followers have little to say about the American revolutionists but devote themselves to scolding the English Whigs. Though the Namierists generally achieve a sophisticated objectivity with regard to persons and parties, they sometimes seem fond of beating the Whigs in order—one suspects—to displease the Whig historians. For example, the unflattering portrait of Charles James Fox that emerges from Richard Pares's brilliant study must surely be read in part as a rebuke to Sir George Otto Trevelyan, or rather to those who have accepted Trevelyan's estimate of Fox. This deflation of Fox and Burke and the other Rockingham Whigs, while accomplished with scarcely a glance in the direction of the colonies, nevertheless deprives the American revolutionists of a group of allies whose high-minded sympathy had been relied upon by earlier historians to help demonstrate the justice of the American cause.

By the same token the righteousness of the Americans is somewhat diminished through the loss of the principal villain in the contest. George III is no longer the foe of liberty, seeking to subvert the British constitution, but an earnest and responsible monarch, doing his job to the best of his abilities. And those abilities, we are told, while not of the highest order, were not small either. George, in fact, becomes a sympathetic figure, and one can scarcely escape the feeling that the Americans were rather beastly to have made things so hard for him.

While the imperial, the economic, and the Namierist approaches have thus contributed in different ways to diminish the prestige of the American Revolution and its promoters, it is a curious fact that none of the ideas has produced any full-scale examination of the Revolution itself or of how it came about. The imperial historians have hitherto been occupied primarily in dissecting the workings of the empire as it existed before the Revolutionary troubles. Although their works have necessarily squinted at the Revolution in every sentence, the only direct confrontations have been brief and inconclusive.

The social and economic interpretation has been applied more extensively to different aspects of the Revolution, but surprisingly enough we still know very little about what the social and economic divisions actually were in most of the colonies and states at the time of the Revolution. Professor Schlesinger's analysis of the role of the merchant class[4] remains a fixed point of knowledge at the opening of the period, and Charles Beard's *Economic Interpretation of the Constitution* is a somewhat shakier foundation at the close of it, reinforced, however, by the work of Merrill Jensen.[5] Historians have bridged the gap between these two points with more assurance than information. There are, it is true, several illuminating studies of local divisions but not enough to warrant any firm conclusions about the role of economic and social forces in the Revolution as a whole. After thirty years we are only a little closer to the materials needed for such conclusions than J. Franklin Jameson was in 1926.

The Namierist approach, as already indicated, has been confined to events in England rather than America. Though the effect of such investigations has been to exonerate George III and discredit the English Whigs, the Revolution has not been a primary issue for Namier or Pares. One student of Professor Namier's, Eric Robson, made a preliminary excursion into the subject but confined his discussion primarily to military history.[6] And while Professor Charles Ritcheson has treated the place of the Revolution in British politics,[7] the implications of Namier's discoveries for developments on this side of the water remain unexplored.

Thus while the new ideas and new discoveries have altered our attitudes toward the American Revolution, they have done so for the most part indirectly, almost surreptitiously, without coming up against the Revolution itself. There is need for intensive and direct examination of all phases of the Revolution in the light of each of these ideas, and we may expect that in the next few years such examinations will be made. Professor Gipson has already begun. I should like to suggest, however, that we need not only to examine

[4] Arthur M. Schlesinger, *The Colonial Merchants and the American Revolution* (New York, 1918).

[5] Merrill Jensen, *The Articles of Confederation* (Madison, Wis., 1940); *The New Nation* (New York, 1950). [Beard's book has now been all but demolished by Robert E. Brown in *Charles Beard and the Constitution* (Princeton, 1956) and by Forrest McDonald in *We, the People* (Chicago, 1958)—Ed.]

[6] Eric Robson, *The American Revolution in its Political and Military Aspects* (London, 1955).

[7] Charles Ritcheson, *British Politics and the American Revolution* (Norman, Okla., 1954).

the Revolution in the light of the ideas but also to re-examine the ideas in the light of the Revolution; and in doing so we need also to examine them in relation to each other.

The Revolution is one of those brute facts which historians must account for, and it is a fact of central importance for ascertaining the meaning and limits of the three ideas we are discussing. I believe that each of the three needs revisions and will take them up in order.

While everyone will acknowledge the importance of the imperial idea and of the discoveries made under its influence, the net effect of that idea has been to emphasize the justice and beneficence of the British imperial system as it existed before the Revolution. May we not therefore pose a question to the imperial historians: if the empire was as fairly administered as you show it to have been, how could the Revolution have happened at all? In their preliminary skirmishes with this problem, imperial historians have frequently implied that the American revolutionists were moved, in part at least, by narrow or selfish views and stirred up by evil-minded agitators. But if historians are to sustain such a view in any full-scale consideration of the Revolution, they face a very difficult task: they must explain men like George Washington, John Adams, Thomas Jefferson, and Benjamin Franklin as agitators or as the dupes of agitators, or as narrow-minded men without the vision to see beyond provincial borders. After all due allowance is made for patriotic myopia, this still seems to me to be an impossible undertaking. Anyone who studies the Revolution can scarcely emerge without some degree of admiration for the breadth of vision that moved these men. In twenty-five years they created a new nation and endowed it with a government that still survives and now has the longest continuous history of any government in existence outside of England. The idea that they were narrow-minded simply will not wash. Nor is it possible to see them as the dupes of their intellectual inferiors. Samuel Adams, Patrick Henry, and James Otis may perhaps be cast as demagogues without seeming out of place, but not the giants of the period. If the British government could not run the empire without bringing on evils that appeared insufferable to men like Washington, Jefferson, John Adams, and Franklin, then the burden of proof would seem to be on those who maintain that it was fit to run an empire.

When the imperial historians are ready to attempt the proof, they must face a second task: they must explain away the character which the Namierist historians have given to the British statesmen of the period. The Namierists, as already indicated, have emphasized the parochial character of English politics in this period. They have cut the Whigs down to size, but they have cut down everyone else on the British political scene likewise. If Parliament was dominated by local interests, what becomes of imperial beneficence and farsightedness?

The whole effect of the Namierist discoveries, so far as the colonies are concerned, must be to show that British statesmen in the 1760's and 1770's, whether in Parliament or in the Privy Council, were too dominated by local interests to be able to run an empire. There was no institution, no party, no organization through which imperial interests, as opposed to strictly British interests, could find adequate expression. In fact the Namierist view and the view of the imperial historians are directly at odds here: though neither group seems as yet to be aware of the conflict, they cannot both be wholly right, and the coming of the Revolution would seem to confirm the Namierist view and to cast doubt on the imperialist one. The achievements of the revolutionists and the failures of the British statesmen suggest in the strongest possible terms that it was the Americans who saw things in the large and the British who wore the blinders. If this is so, may it not be that the case for the beneficence and justice of the British Empire before the Revolution has been overstated?

In response to our argument *ad hominem* the imperialists may summon the aid of the economic interpretation to show that the Americans, however high-toned their arguments, were really moved by economic considerations of the basest kind. We may, however, call these considerations basic rather than base and offer our previous character witnesses against the economists too. There is no time to plead to every indictment here, but one may perhaps answer briefly the strongest yet offered, that of Charles Beard, and then suggest how the economic interpretation needs revision. Though Beard expressly disclaimed that his economic interpretation was the whole story, he gave not merely a one-sided view but a false one. All the evidence that Beard extracted from the records of the Constitutional Convention points toward the sordid conclusion that the delegates who held public securities also held undemocratic political views, motivated consciously or unconsciously by the desire to protect their investments. Beard consistently overlooked contradictory evidence. I will cite only two examples.

The first is his treatment of Roger Sherman, the delegate to the Constitutional Convention from Connecticut. Sherman, he notes, had risen from poverty to affluence and held nearly eight thousand dollars worth of public securities. Sherman's corresponding political philosophy he represents by the following statement: "Roger Sherman believed in reducing the popular influence in the new government to the minimum. When it was proposed that the members of the first branch of the national legislature should be elected, Sherman said that he was 'opposed to the election by the people, insisting that it ought to be by the state legislatures. The people, he said, immediately should have as little to do as may be about the government. They want information and are constantly liable to be misled.' "[8]

The quotation certainly supports Beard's view, but Beard failed to indicate what Sherman said at other times in the convention. On June 4, four days after the speech Beard quotes, Sherman was against giving the President a veto power, because he "was against enabling any one man to stop the will of the whole. No one man could be found so far above all the rest in wisdom." On June 21 he argued again for election of the House of Representatives by the state legislatures, but after election by the people had been decided upon, spoke for annual elections as against triennial, because "He thought the representatives ought to return home and mix with the people." On August 14 he was in favor of substantial pay for congressmen, because otherwise "men ever so fit could not serve unless they were at the same time rich."[9] Whatever explanation may be offered for these views, they suggest a much broader confidence in the people than might be inferred from the single remark by which Beard characterized the man.

It cannot be said that the statements which Beard neglected are concerned with an aspect of Sherman's views not relevant to the

[8] Charles Beard, *An Economic Interpretation of the Constitution of the United States* (New York, 1913), pp. 213-14.

[9] *Records of the Federal Convention of 1787,* ed. Max Farrand (New Haven, 1911-37), I, 99, 362; II, 291.

problem Beard was examining: they are certainly as relevant as the statement he did quote. His treatment of Pierce Butler, the delegate from South Carolina, is similar. Beard notes that Butler held public securities and that he argued for apportionment of representation according to wealth.[10] He neglects to mention that Butler, in spite of his security holdings, opposed full payment of the public debt, "lest it should compel payment as well to the Blood-suckers who had speculated on the distresses of others, as to those who had fought and bled for their country." [11] The statement is relevant, but directly opposed, to Beard's thesis.

It requires only a reading of the Convention debates to see that Beard's study needs revision.[12] But the trouble with the economic interpretation, as currently applied to the whole Revolutionary period, goes deeper. The trouble lies in the assumption that a conflict between property rights and human rights has been the persistent theme of American history from the beginning. It was undoubtedly the great theme of Beard's day, and Beard was on the side of human rights, where decent men belong in such a conflict. From the vantage point of twentieth-century Progressivism, he lined up the members of the Constitutional Convention, found their pockets stuffed with public securities, and concluded that they were on the wrong side.

It was a daring piece of work, and it fired the imagination of Beard's fellow progressives.[13] Vernon L. Parrington has recorded how it "struck home like a submarine torpedo—the discovery that the drift toward plutocracy was not a drift away from the spirit of the Constitution, but an inevitable unfolding from its premises." As a result of Beard's work, Parrington was able to see that "From the beginning . . . democracy and property had been at bitter odds." [14]

[10] Beard, *Economic Interpretation,* pp. 81-2, 192.

[11] Farrand, *Records, II,* 392.

[12] Robert E. Brown's *Charles Beard and the Constitution* (Princeton, 1956) appeared too late to be of use in preparation of this paper, but the reader will find in it abundant additional evidence of deficiencies in Beard's use of the Convention records.

[13] See Douglas Adair, "The Tenth Federalist Revisited," *William and Mary Quarterly,* 3d Ser., VIII (1951), 48-67; Richard Hofstadter, "Beard and the Constitution: The History of an Idea," *American Quarterly,* II (1950), 195-213.

[14] Vernon L. Parrington, *Main Currents in American Thought* (New York, 1927-30), III, 410.

Parrington went on to construct his own image of American history in these terms, and he too had a powerful influence. Together he and Beard virtually captured the American past for Progressivism, a performance all the more remarkable when we consider that they did not enlist the revered founding fathers of the Constitution on their side.

It is time, however, that we had another look at the conflict between human rights and property rights; and the Revolutionary period is a good place to begin, for however strong the conflict may later have become, it was not a dominant one then. Anyone who studies the Revolution must notice at once the attachment of all articulate Americans to property. "Liberty and Property" was their cry, not "Liberty and Democracy." In the face of the modern dissociation of property from liberty, historians have often felt that this concern of the revolutionists for property was a rather shabby thing, and that the constitutional principles so much talked of, before 1776 as well as afterward, were invented to hide it under a more attractive cloak. But the Americans were actually quite shameless about their concern for property and made no effort to hide it, because it did not seem at all shabby to them. The colonial protests against taxation frankly and openly, indeed passionately, affirm the sanctity of property. And the passion is not the simple and unlovely passion of greed. For eighteenth-century Americans, property and liberty were one and inseparable, because property was the only foundation yet conceived for security of life and liberty: without security for his property, it was thought, no man could live or be free except at the mercy of another.

The revolutionists' coupling of property with life and liberty was not an attempt to lend respectability to property rights, nor was it an attempt to enlist the masses in a struggle for the special privileges of a small wealthy class. Property in eighteenth-century America was not associated with special privilege, as it came to be for later generations. Land was widely owned. A recent investigation has demonstrated that in Massachusetts, a key state in the Revolution, nearly every adult male could meet the property qualifications for the franchise.[15] We hear much from modern historians about the propertyless masses of the Revolutionary period,

[15] Robert E. Brown, *Middle-Class Democracy and the Revolution in Massachusetts, 1691-1780* (Ithaca, N. Y., 1955).

but it is altogether improbable that the mass of Americans were without property.

The Americans fought England because Parliament threatened the security of property. They established state constitutions with property qualifications for voting and officeholding in order to protect the security of property. And when the state governments seemed inadequate to the task, they set up the Federal government for the same purpose. The economic motive was present in all these actions, but it was present as the friend of universal liberty. Devotion to security of property was not the attitude of a privileged few but the fundamental principle of the many, inseparable from everything that went by the name of freedom and adhered to the more fervently precisely because it did affect most people so intimately.

What we have done in our social and economic interpretations of the Revolution is to project into eighteenth-century America a situation which existed in the nineteenth and early twentieth centuries, when property and the means of production became concentrated in the hands of a few, when liberty if it was to exist at all had to get along not only without the aid of property but in opposition to it. We seem now to be approaching a period when property, in another form, may again be widely distributed and may again become the friend rather than the enemy of liberty. Whether such is the case or not, as historians we should stop projecting into the eighteenth century the particular economic and social antagonisms that we have found in later generations. We may still believe that the American Revolution was in part a contest about who should rule at home, but we should beware of assuming that people took sides in that contest according to whether or not they owned property. And we should totally abandon the assumption that those who showed the greatest concern for property rights were not devoted to human rights.

The challenge of the Revolution to the Namier school of historians is less direct and less crucial, but it does pose one or two questions which these historians seem not to have confronted. The first is whether the new judgment of George III has not raised that monarch's reputation a little too high. Granted that George was neither the fool nor the knave he has hitherto been thought, granted that he was moved by a desire to maintain parliamentary supremacy rather than regal supremacy, it is nevertheless true that under his leadership England lost an important, if not the most important, part of her empire. The loss was not inevitable. All the objectives of the Americans before 1776 could have been attained within the empire, and would have cost the mother country little or nothing. George undoubtedly received a good deal of assistance from other politicians in losing the colonies, but the contention of the Namierists has been that the king still held a position of central responsibility in the British government in the 1760's and 1770's, a responsibility which they have shown that he shouldered and carried. If he was responsible then he must be held responsible. He must bear most of the praise or blame for the series of measures that alienated and lost the colonies, and it is hard to see how there can be much praise.

The other question that the Revolution poses for the Namierists may be more fundamental. Virtually no one in British politics, they argue, had any political principles that reached beyond local or factional interests. The argument, though convincingly presented, presumes a consistent hypocrisy or delusion on the part of the Whig opposition. It may be that the Whigs were hypocritical in their attack on George III and their support of the Americans. But if so why were they hypocritical in just the way they were? Why did they appeal to principles of government that later won acceptance? Can we be sure that it was only in order to attack their opponents? Can we be sure they were on the right side for the wrong reasons? I do not pretend to know the answers to these questions, but I am not quite comfortable about judgments of history in which people are condemned for being prematurely antimonarchical.

What I would suggest in conclusion is that the Whig interpretation of the American Revolution may not be as dead as some historians would have us believe, that George Bancroft may not have been so far from the mark as we have often assumed. Is it not time to ask again a few of the old questions that he was trying to answer? Let us grant that local interests were the keynote of British politics; we must still ask: how did the Americans, living on the edge of empire, develop the breadth of vision and the attachment to principle which they displayed in that remarkable period from 1763 to 1789? While English politics remained parochial and the empire was dissolving for lack of vision, how did the Americans generate the forces that carried them into a new nationality and a new human liberty?

The answer, I think, may lie in a comparatively neglected field of American scholarship. During the past fifty years our investigations of the colonial period have been directed primarily by the imperial idea and the social and economic one. We have seen the colonists as part of the empire or else we have seen them as the pawns of sweeping economic and social forces. What we have neglected is the very thing that the English have been pursuing in the study of their institutions. We have neglected, comparatively speaking at least, the study of local institutions, and it is in such a study that we may perhaps discover the answer to the fundamental question that moved Bancroft, the question of how a great nation with great principles of freedom was forged from thirteen quarrelsome colonies. What kind of institutions produced a Jefferson, a Madison, a Washington, a John Adams? Not imperial institutions certainly. The imperial machinery had no place for Americans except in performing local services. No American ever sat on the Board of Trade or the Privy Council. Few Americans ever came in contact with imperial officers. It was in local American institutions that these men gained their political experience.

Two generations ago Herbert Baxter Adams thought he had the clue to the question of where American liberty began, and he put a host of graduate students to work studying the local institutions of the colonies. As we all know, they did not find precisely what Adams was looking for, but they produced a prodigious number of studies, which are still the principal source of historical information about many colonial institutions. Some have been superseded by more recent scholarship, but we need more new studies of this kind, which will take advantage of what we have learned since Adams's time about the imperial setting and about social and economic forces.

We need to know how the individual's picture of society was formed. We need to study the social groupings in every colony: towns, plantations, counties, churches, schools, clubs, and other groups which occupied the social horizons of the individual colonist. We need to study political parties and factions in every colony. We need to study the way government worked at the local level. We need to study the county courts and the justices of the peace. We need to study the distribution of land and other forms of wealth from decade to decade and from place to place. We need to know so elementary a thing as the history of representation and the history of taxation in every colony. We have always known that the Revolution had something to do with the phrase, "no taxation without representation," and yet, after two generations of modern scholarship, how many scholars have studied the history of taxation in the colonies? Who really knows anything about the history of representation?

Without abandoning what we have gained from the imperial idea and from economic interpretations, we must dissect the local institutions which produced the American Revolution, the institutions from which were distilled the ideas that enabled men of that age to stand as the architects of modern liberty. The task has not been wholly neglected. A number of scholars have been quietly working at it. I will not attempt to name them here, but their discoveries are sufficient to show that this is the direction which scholarship in colonial history should now take and that the rewards will not be small.

SUGGESTED ADDITIONAL READING

The most notable of the early histories of the Revolution, apart from David Ramsay's, was William Gordon's *History of the Rise, Progress, and Establishment of the Independence of the United States of America* (4 vols., London, 1788). This has long been discredited as little more than a plagiarism from the *Annual Register;* but Gordon, a Roxbury clergyman and patriot, did have access to a mass of official papers, which he sometimes used. His history, especially the first volume, is worth study for that reason. It is the closest thing to an official history that was produced by the Revolutionary generation, though Gordon published it in England and evidently tempered his interpretations to suit his British audience, thereby offending his original sponsors.

The fullest statement of the so-called "Whig interpretation" is still George Bancroft's *History of the United States* (10 vols., Boston, 1834-74), even though Bancroft, a Jacksonian Democrat, would have repudiated the label "Whig" because of its connotations of the American party of that name. More appropriately designated as "Whig" is George Otto Trevelyan's *The American Revolution* (4 vols., New York, 1898-1907), easily the most literate history of the Revolution.

The first revisions of the Whig interpretation coincided with the rapprochement between England and America at the opening of the twentieth century. A piece of revisionism comparable to that of C. K. Adams was Sydney George Fisher's "The Legendary and Mythmaking Process in Histories of the American Revolution" (American Philosophical Society, *Proceedings,* LI [1912], 53-75).

Arthur M. Schlesinger in his *New Viewpoints in American History* (New York, 1922) offered a general statement of the new perspective. The same revisionist approach prompted the first scholarly and sympathetic study of the Loyalists: C. H. Van Tyne's *The Loyalists in the American Revolution* (New York, 1902). A more recent study, also sympathetic, is William H. Nelson, *The American Tory* (Oxford, 1961).

Among the "Imperial" School of historians, Charles McLean Andrews gave a very thoughtful consideration of the Revolution in his *Colonial Background of the American Revolution* (New Haven, 1924). He also expressed his views in "The American Revolution: An Interpretation" (*American Historical Review,* XXXI [1926], 219-32). Andrews was the most learned colonial historian of his day, and the wisdom of his observations extends well beyond the limits of any single school of thought. A book which originated in the Imperialist approach but offers a novel and important interpretation of how the Revolution was precipitated is O. M. Dickerson, *The Navigation Acts and the American Revolution* (Philadelphia, 1951). Professor Gipson's interpretation will receive full expression in the concluding volumes of his *British Empire before the American Revolution.*

The Namierist school of history has produced very little that bears directly on the Revolution. Namier himself published a book called *England in the Age of the American Revolution,* and Charles Ritcheson one called *British Politics and the American Revolution,* but the focus of attention in both is British politics rather than the Revolution. Eric Robson's book, from which a selection is given above, has been reprinted by the Shoe String Press (Hamden, Conn., 1965).

The social and economic interpretation has had numerous expressions, mostly devoted to particular aspects of the subject. Notable among them are A. M. Schlesinger, *The Colonial Merchants and the American Revolution* (New York, 1918); Merrill Jensen, *The Articles of Confederation* (Madison, Wisconsin, 1940) and *The New Nation* (New York, 1950). Clarence Ver Steeg in "The American Revolution Considered as an Economic Movement" (*Huntington Library Quarterly,* XX [1957], 361-72), suggests a number of areas where the economic forces at work in the Revolution have not yet been examined. Frederick B. Tolles discusses the scholarship which has tested some of Jameson's propositions in "The American Revolution Considered as a Social Movement: A Re-evaluation" (*American Historical Review,* LIX [1954], 1-12).

Daniel J. Boorstin's interpretation may be compared with a variety of studies of the reasoning by which the colonists justified their resistance to England. Carl Becker emphasized the influence of the Enlightenment in *The Declaration of Independence* (New York, 1922). Clinton Rossiter stresses the influence of earlier colonial institutions and ideas in *Seedtime of the Republic* (New York, 1953). I have discussed the constitutional arguments of the 1760s in *The Stamp Act Crisis* (with Helen M. Morgan, Chapel Hill, 1953). C. H. McIlwain in *The American Revolution* (New York, 1923) and R. L. Schuyler in *Parliament and the British Empire* (New York 1929) give differing views of the colonists' later constitutional position. Caroline Robbins in *The Eighteenth Century Commonwealthman* (Cambridge, Mass., 1959) identifies a British political tradition that influenced Americans; and Bernard Bailyn in the Introduction to *Pamphlets of the American Revolution,* volume I (Cambridge, Mass., 1965) spells out the ways in which that tradition affected American Revolutionary thought. A new intellectual dimension, the religious, is given the Revolution in Carl Bridenbaugh's *Mitre and Sceptre* (New York, 1962), which shows that fear of an Anglican episcopal establishment antagonized many Americans against England. The influence of the New England clergy in bringing on the Revolution had previously been suggested in Alice Baldwin's *New England Clergy and the American Revolution* (Durham, N. C., 1928). Miss Baldwin emphasized the role of the clergy as purveyors of John Locke's political theory. Perry Miller gives the more characteristically American religious ideas an important function in Revolutionary thought in "From the Covenant to the Revival" in J. W. Smith, ed., *The Shaping of American Religion* (Princeton, 1961).

My own view of the Revolution is stated in *The Birth of the Republic* (Chicago, 1956). Since the address on "Revisions in Need of Revising," a number of studies have appeared, some which would seem to support the points made in it and some of which have the effect of raising doubts about them. Beard's *Economic Interpretation of the Constitution* has been effectively refuted by Robert E. Brown's *Charles Beard and the Constitution* (Princeton,

1956) and Forrest McDonald's *We the People* (Chicago, 1958). Lee Benson in *Turner and Beard* (Glencoe, Ill., 1960), Merrill Jensen in "Democracy and the American Revolution," *Huntington Library Quarterly*, XX [1957], 321-41, J. T. Main in *The Antifederalists* (Chapel Hill, 1961), and E. J. Ferguson in *The Power of the Purse* (Chapel Hill, 1961) all contribute insights and information that directly or indirectly tend to support some of Beard's assumptions about the economic and social forces at work in the Revolutionary period. Herbert Butterfield has mounted an attack on Namier in *George III and the Historians* (New York, 1959). Bernhard Knollenberg in *Origin of the American Revolution 1759-1766* (New York, 1960) emphasizes the variety of causes that irritated the colonists in those years.

Several new studies of the Revolution in particular states and regions have appeared. One of the most notable, David S. Lovejoy, *Rhode Island Politics and the American Revolution 1760-1776*, shows that Rhode Islanders, though divided into political factions on local issues, were not much troubled by class conflict and were generally united on the large question of hostility to British taxation. On the other hand, Staughton Lynd in *Antifederalism in Dutchess County, New York* (Chicago, 1962) shows that in that area at least, class conflict did affect the Revolution. An important study bearing on the urban origins of the Revolution is Carl Bridenbaugh's *Cities in Revolt* (New York, 1955). John R. Alden, *The South in the Revolution* (Baton Rouge, 1957) and Jack P. Greene, *The Quest for Power* (Chapel Hill, 1963) are both important for an understanding of the Revolution in the South.

The Classics in History Series

DRIFT AND MASTERY, Walter Lippmann,
introduction and notes by William E. Leuchtenburg—S-CH-2

EMPIRE AND NATION: John Henry Dickinson's
"Letters from a Farmer in Pennsylvania"
and Richard Henry Lee's "Letters from the Federal Farmer,"—S-CH-5

FRONTIER AND SECTION: Selected Essays
of Frederick Jackson Turner,
introduction by Ray Allen Billington—S-CH-1

HISTORY OF THE UNITED STATES DURING THE ADMINISTRATIONS
OF JEFFERSON AND MADISON, Henry Adams,
abridged and edited by George Dangerfield and Otey M. Scruggs.
Vol. I: Jefferson—S-CH-9, Vol. II: Madison—S-CH-10

THE NEW FREEDOM, Woodrow Wilson,
introduction and notes by William E. Leuchtenburg—S-CH-4

THE NEW NATIONALISM, Theodore Roosevelt,
introduction and notes by William E. Leuchtenburg—S-CH-3

SOCIAL DARWINISM: Selected Essays of William Graham Sumner,
edited by Stow Persons—S-CH-7

THE SUPREME COURT AND THE CONSTITUTION, Charles A. Beard,
introduction by Alan F. Westin—S-CH-6

WEALTH VS. COMMONWEALTH, Henry D. Lloyd,
edited by Thomas C. Cochran—S-CH-8